I0138615

NeverEnding Maddness

A GIRL LOST TO THE WORLD

FROST & FLAME TRILOGY BOOK 3

BY RICK KUEBER

STELLIUM BOOKS
Grant Park, Illinois 60940

i

Neverending Maddness: A Girl Lost to the World
is the third book of the Frost & Flame Trilogy
of fictional books by Rick Kueber.
These books are, however, based on true events.

www.stelliumbooks.com
Copyright 2015 © Rick Kueber
All rights reserved
First published 2015
Manufactured in the United States
ISBN:978-0692533260

Dedications

For my team- Jenn, Katie, and Theo: I am blessed to have a team with more character and unique personalities than I could have dreamed up. Without you, these adventures would not have been the same.

Thank You

For my true friends, the list is too long to name you all, and my family: You have all been very encouraging and supportive and always been there when I needed you. Thank You

For my son Daniel, who is growing into an amazing young man:

You have encouraged me to follow my dreams without question, and I hope I have done the same for you. You have always been my greatest adventure. Do what makes you happy in life, be inspired to make others happy, and live your dreams.

Love always, Dad

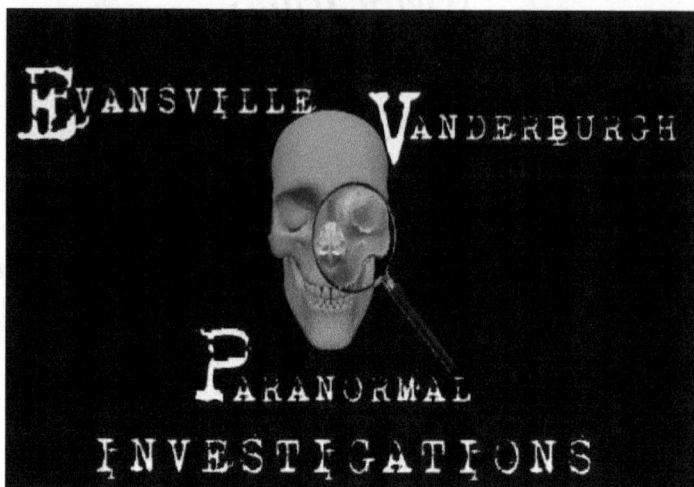

EVANSVILLE VANDERBURGH
PARANORMAL
INVESTIGATIONS

*Background Image Art &
Cover Model Photography: Hilary Lee*

Book Cover Design: Annette Munnich

Location Photography: Angela Makeever

Cover Model: Miranda Lee Hoyt (Maddie)

Additional thanks to those who shared this adventure with the EVP team and a special acknowledgment to those who are referred to in the contents of this book:

Mike Lee

Hilary Lee

Tabitha Linton

NeverEnding

Maddness

By Rick Kueber

Edited by: Cinda Payne Inman

Copyright© September 1, 2015 – R.J. Kueber
All Rights Reserved. Except as provided by the copyright act, [date, etc.] no part of this publication may be reproduced, stored in a retrieval system or transmitted in any form or by any means without permission

NeverEnding Maddness is a novel based on actual and fictional events, documented history and investigations. Though the main characters in this book are based on real people, their names and specifics have been altered because there are elements of fiction throughout this literary work and is not intended to be a complete or accurate account. The team members of Evansville Vanderburgh Paranormal Investigations, and Psychic/Mediums- Theo Kostaridis are portrayed as themselves, and a short bio on each has been included-

Photo by Grace Kirsch

CHAPTER INDEX

Prologue:

My team had been together for a few years and had been on every kind of paranormal investigation imaginable. Over the past few years we had investigated three of the most incredible cases I could have ever even dreamed of. The families and the lost souls we had helped had given us a true sense of purpose to go along with our passion. We were truly blessed in that respect.

The first phenomenal case was that of a little ghost girl named Ashley Sue Helmach. She was a poor child who had been outcast by her community in the late 1800's and eventually her only family had even turned their back on her. She had been burned as a witch child because of her differences, and that alone was tragic, but our encounters with her spirit and the tale we had uncovered were almost more tragic than we could bear. Though it was a nightmarish investigation, we struggled our way through it, and had become better people for having not given up on the desperate and confused spirit of this child. Even now, the spirit of young Ash, visits my team and I, and has even been known to visit those who have read her story.

The second amazing case we had been involved in was an incredible mystery and surprise to all of us. A group of young brothers who had died at a very young age, and a few not so nice spirits haunted a local establishment. With the aid of another renowned psychic, we researched and investigated a local private club known as the Owls Nest. The experiences there were unbelievable and with the help of little Ashley Sue, our ghostly friend, we were able to help these child spirits, as well some of those that had lived with or been touched by their presence and even their absence.

The third and possibly most active and frightening case involved numerous spirits, with one in particular, and our endeavors to help them. This is their story...

ix

CHAPTER 1
FORGOTTEN

The young girl was awakened from her dreams by the rustling of crispy brown leaves and the snapping of a brittle branch which had long been dead. Her legs were curled up and wrapped tightly within the heavy, cotton fabric of her torn dress and her face and fingers were pained. One side of her face was pocked with the marks of laying against the hard ground and crisp dry leaves of a pin oak, while the other side and her fingers stung from the night's frosty air having nipped at them over the past several hours.

The sudden noise had startled her from sleep and a flurry of frightening possibilities poured through her thoughts. Still not quite awake, she leaped to her feet and spun around, her eyes searching the forest for the origin of the sounds. Bewildered and terrified, she began to briskly walk away from where she imagined the sound came from. Her strides increased to a jog and then an all-out run as her fears intensified with every step. As she ran through the lifeless wilderness, the girl shot glances over her shoulders as often as she could, fearing the worst. Had the devil's child followed her? She was certain that it had, and that it only taunted her from a distance to drive her insane from fright. It knew her secret. It must have a plan to torture and torment her, just as it had been tortured.

She knew it was her doing that caused this, though it was not her intention. In fact, when she had revealed the truth about this devil child, it was only to shift the glaring eyes of her elders from her and onto another. Now, she would pay dearly for betraying what was once a friend. How she wished that she could return to that day and time to change her past, and inevitably change her present and future, but she knew, all too well, that this was not possible.

After days of stumbling aimlessly through the forest with little to drink and only a few dead berries to eat, she began to feel not only exhausted as she ran, but weak and dizzy. Her blistered feet carried her unknowingly onto a seldom traveled road where she collapsed. The young girl's body was limp, bruised and dirty. Her dress was torn, boots scuffed, and her hair was a tangled mess, when a wagon, drawn by a single black steed, turned the corner. The driver spotted her straightaway and 'whoa'd his horse to a stop. The steam snorted out of the horse's flaring nostrils and contrasted sharply with the sheen of its ebony coat.

The dawn was breaking through the foggy morning, as the driver dismounted his wagon, and rushed to where the girl laid motionless. He pulled his wide brimmed hat down tight against his head. Squinting his eyes, he peered side to side and listened closely in all directions. Swiftly he scooped up the young lady and without hesitation, placed her in the back of his wagon, covering her completely with an old, worn, wool horse blanket. Retaking his seat, he snapped the reigns and the wagon was off with a start. Though she was unconscious, some part of her knew she was no longer traveling alone, and while it gave her some comfort, she would soon realize that the nightmare of this devil's child would only be the beginning of her troubles. Her peace of mind, her trust in mankind, and her sanity were already beginning their departure, making way for an influx of veritable madness.

2

Nearly three days had passed when the girl's eyes opened again. A blurry, orange glow danced about and the onset of confusion began. Her malnourished body was still weak and pained, and her eyelids lifted for only seconds at a time. They felt heavy and stiff and it took an effort to move them. She drew a deep and labored breath, tensing and relaxing her body to extremes, which caused a gravelly whimper as she exhaled. A frightening realization overtook her as she forced her eyes open again and the yellowy, orange light flickered and grew brighter...FIRE. Despite her discomfort, she jerked backwards and let out the slightest of a shriek.

"Oh, deary! Madison! You've awakened!" a tender and aged female voice answered her shriek.

A large figure moved towards her and her vision began to clear. The new surroundings were becoming recognizable as the blurred lines became crisp. She had found herself in a small room, lit only by the dusky light that filtered in through a tiny window just above the bed she had been sleeping in. Directly across from her, the opposite wall, not six or seven feet away, a fire roared in a small brick fireplace. The only other decor in the room was a sturdy, yet crudely made chair and hand-hewn table, where the large figure, a very rosy-cheeked, old woman, had been sitting.

"Where am I?" She asked. The raspy words ached in her dry throat.

"Don't you worry your pretty little head dear." The kind voice said as she crossed the room and handed her a small tin cup of water. She took a large gulp and swallowed it with some difficulty. "Slow down little Madison. There is more water to be had, if you wish."

She sipped at the tiny tin cup slowly, feeling every drop saturating her tongue and soothing her throat. It seeped in, like rain into the dry, cracked earth, rejuvenating the life within her. It was odd that the grand-motherly woman called her by the name Madison twice since she had awakened. She had no recollection of this woman, who she was, or how

3

she knew her name. At this moment, it was the least of her worries. In her mind, the worrisome thoughts flew in and out like fluttering moths to a torchlight. She yearned for her old life, but despised the thought of returning to the home and family that had ruined her life. Who was this elderly woman, and why was she caring for her? Was this woman truly as kindhearted as she seemed, or would this too be revealed to be a cruel lie? She had no idea where she was. Her last memory was of being only a few days walk from her home, her town, her old life, but now, she could be anywhere. She was lost.

The woman took the cup from the girl's frail hands and refilled it from a small pitcher that sat on the table. Placing the tin cup on the floor near the bed, the old woman spoke softly.

"Rest now, child. I will bring some soup and bread when I return shortly." Her head dropped and she glanced briefly toward the tattered young woman as she opened the door and swiftly departed the room, closing the door behind her...

~****~

My time away from paranormal research and investigating, how ever short, was truly needed. I had taken the time to regain my own self. I was reconnecting with the person I had been, once, not such a long time ago. Time with my son, Daniel, was no longer distracted by the fears of my experiences and the theories of current supernatural happenings. We had our time together, one on one, and it was complete...and it was beautiful...and it was ours. No one, and no thing, could ever take that from us.

It was early April and while it was still rather cool, it had warmed up more than normal on this particular Saturday. A warmer than average spring day had transformed into a dark and sultry evening. Clouds gathered and kept the stars and moon hidden from sight. I was not spending this weekend with my boy and late that night, while trolling the internet and catching up on social media, my cell phone rang. I did not

4

recognize the out of state number, but I answered anyway.

"Hello?" I answered the unknown caller.

"Hi, is this Rick?" The woman on the other end said.

"Yes it is. Can I help you?" I kept my professional tone until I could figure out who I was talking to.

"It's Hilary. Remember me from the conventions?" she said lightly.

"Hilary! How have you been?" I did remember her, a sweet young woman who was raising money to save a wonderfully historic landmark near her home town... in northern Ohio.

"Been pretty good... okay, look... I know we both know hundreds of people, famous and not so famous, in the paranormal field... but I really want you and your team to help me out here if you can." She wasn't exactly beating around the bush, but she hadn't gotten to the point yet either.

"What can we do for you?" I expected her to ask for help with a fund-raiser, or something like that.

"It's Maddie...Madison...she has gotten worse and I can't handle her anymore... I can't even bring myself to go to the 'Infirmary' alone now. There is no real rush... she's been waiting a hundred years, but if you think you could pencil us in, we could really use your team's expertise." Her voice was troubled.

"Send me what you have... everything... history, photos, time lines, whatever you have managed to dig up, and if you need help with that, let me know and one or two of us will come and work with you. Once we have that in hand, we can put a plan together." Hilary had often referenced the woman haunting the Infirmary as 'Maddie', this much I already knew. I also knew this was a serious situation, just from the sound of her voice as she spoke about it.

"Thank you so much! I won't keep you, and I'll be in touch via

5

email, in the next few weeks, okay?" Hilary, once again, asked for confirmation that we would be willing to help.

"Of course! Just email, or call, or whatever you need to do. We're here for you." I meant every word I said, but part of me was honestly worried.

When the conversation ended, I sat on the edge of my bed deep in thought, considering what another out of state investigation would mean to the team, and to my son. I made the definitive decision that no matter how dire the paranormal need, my son would come first. Knowing that, I was able to begin to focus on postulating a plan. Step one, as always, was to assemble the team and make them aware that we would be having another long distance investigation.

***

It took a bit of planning, re-planning, and rescheduling, but before long we had a team meeting set. Like most, this meeting was at the Starbucks inside of our local Barnes & Noble Booksellers store. Our chatter rambled for quite some time about family and friends and the reappearance of the ground, after a long and white winter, but mostly about Katie's new little boy, and how difficult and stressful parenting could be. Jenn and I tried to give her comforting advise, but Theo just sat back blushing and grinned.

"I have no idea about being a parent, and I don't plan on ever having an idea about it." He chuckled knowing his lifestyle had taken that possibility out of the equation. "But, I think you will make a wonderful mom."

"Well, no sense in prolonging the inevitable." I said, and stopped the conversation cold. "We have another investigation request... in Northern Ohio."

All eyes turned to me, and mouths dropped open. Even though there were mostly complaints about taking a break, I knew it would be a shock to the system to jump back in to investigating 'with both feet'. It was obvious to the team that this case must be important, and someone must be in dire need, for me to suggest trekking to northern Ohio.

"When do we go?" was the first question that was asked...by Katie, who smiled.

"I haven't set it up yet, but there is apparently no rush, so we can probably do some research and planning before we have to set a date. Theo, Jenn... are you two on board?" I asked, already knowing the answers.

"Uh.... nah... I'm just going to sit this one out." Jenn replied calmly.

"Really?" I asked, both confused and concerned.

"DUH! Set it up! You know I'm in!" Jenn's sarcasm had, for the first time in a while, surfaced and caught me off guard. We all laughed at how I had fallen for her comment, hook, line and sinker.

"Just let me know ahead of time so I can schedule the time off, but you know I'll be there." Theo said, still laughing a bit between words.

"It's settled then. I'll contact Hilary and let her know, and then we'll have another meeting to plan a schedule, probably in a couple of weeks." I sat back in my chair and sipped at my French vanilla cappuccino.

"No rest for the wicked." Katie said jokingly.

"Or us..." I mumbled under my breath.

We stayed in contact every few days, even if only by text messages. I had moved into the modern day, and using my phone for messaging and social media became something that was second nature to me. Just a few short years ago, no one would have ever believed it, but here I was...smartphone in hand, sending group text messages, and posting to Facebook on the go. Over the next couple of weeks, I had received text messages alerting me to newly discovered historical documents which Hilary would then share with me via email. Although I had several desktop computers in the team office and my laptop, I preferred to print out the documents, and make hard-copies for the team to look at.

Our next planned meeting on Sunday afternoon finally arrived. I wandered into the Barnes & Noble and took an immediate right turn. The store was abuzz with shoppers and bookworms of all shapes and sizes. Avoiding them all, I made a bee-line for the Starbucks. A Grande French vanilla latte had been ordered, and I chose one of several empty booths to hold our meeting. As I awaited the barista to call my name, I thought about what this new case could develop into. I had a manila file folder with the original email, three document print outs, and copies of each. I gently placed it on the table and laid my hand on top of it, as if it held top secret information and some foreign spy was about to sneak up and whisk it away. The thought made me smile, and as I pondered the difference in the dangers we faced, versus those of espionage, the twenty-something woman with a pierced nose and intentionally unkempt hair called my name to alert me of the arrival of my sweet, caffeinated heaven. I pushed the file folder to the far end of the booth and quickly retrieved my piping hot beverage. I hadn't been sipping my latte very long when the trio burst into the bookstore in a clambering conversation, and spying me tossed waves in my direction and took their place in line to order drinks of their own. Theo was the first to slide into the booth directly across from where I sat in silence. Jenn took her seat next to me, and Katie slid in across from her.

"So...whatcha got there?" Jenn broke the momentary silence before we had even said hello.

"I suppose there's no reason to wait." I said as I opened the folder and passed out paper-clipped copies of the documents I had received. "Here's the first things I have from Hilary."

Even though I was familiar to the letter with each page, all four of us began studying the first two-page document. It was only a financial and statistical report from 1888, but it did give us some insight on the harsh realities of the Infirmary. Money went much farther in the nineteenth century, but even by those standards, there was scarcely enough to maintain a facility of this size...much less afford any comforts or proper care of those within its walls.

"Interesting..." Mumbled Theo. It was the only comment until the second document was reached and everyone began reading. This scanned page was a continuation of a multi-page document, and at the end of several paragraphs detailing the history and function of the poor house and infirmary, was this simple, yet chilling statement: "There is a cemetery next to the infirmary. Most of the markers are gone. Following is a partial list of Infirmary deaths from 1890-1910. Eyes widened as pages turned. Alphabetically listed, the names and minor details were listed in two columns, and ran for pages and pages.

"Holy crap!" Katie finally exclaimed. "How many people died at this place?"

"I know right?" Theo responded. "I can't count that high." It was a comment of morbid humor, but it was not far from accurate.

"No wonder this place is haunted. There must've been hundreds of deaths there. And to have put so many people into unmarked graves and just forget about them." Jenn's words were resoundingly obvious.

"I agree, Jenn, it's tragic to think so many people could have been forgotten by their families, mourned by only other discarded souls, non-existent to the world..." I paused, as sorrow took me for a brief moment, "and from what Hilary has told me, there are two unmarked cemeteries on the property besides this one. I can only imagine how many different spirits may occupy the old infirmary, but there *is* one in particular that needs our help."

The sound of shuffling papers and curious mutterings filled the air between us. Our sounds settled down and the ramblings of all of the surrounding shoppers began to overtake our own. The silence at our table was brought on by the final piece of documentation that had been distributed. Color copies of a much yellowed property map and basic floor plan of the infirmary drew everyone's attention. Small stains and smudges, discolored creases and wear and tear created by age and use adorned the scanned copies and gave them all of the mystery and intrigue of a newly discovered pirate's treasure map.

"Geez!" Theo said, rubbing his forehead. "This place is huge. Is this one story, or is there a basement, or what?" It was a valid question, as the floor plan only mapped out the first floor.

"Well..." I sheepishly began, "It's actually four stories, but I honestly don't know about any basement. I guess there could be one."

"Well, hell! A place this big...times four, hundreds of deaths, and you think there is one spirit there that needs our help? What the hell makes you think that?" Jenn was being brutally honest and bitterly sarcastic all at the same time.

"Why?" I paused, trying to reason why I should take someone's word over the logic of my most trusted teammate. "This is why..." While everyone studied the maps in front of them, I removed the last printout from the folder. "This is the email that came with the documents we have just looked at. Between the phone call I had with Hilary and this..." I trailed off before beginning to read the email aloud.

" *Rick,*

Here are the first documents I have uncovered, but I know there are many more. I'm going to try not to send anything that isn't relevant. I'll have more in a few days. Have the girls call me and I'll see if they can help sort through it.

Had another disturbing dream last night. They're getting worse. I remember feeling very cold, like I was literally freezing, and there were people ripping the skin off of me. There was breaking glass and the feeling of falling (which I have dreamed about before). I know that sounds like a ball of terrifying B.S., but it's mostly just like fuzzy glimpses of memory, but those things were definitely part of the dream...it started out that way. Then I remember standing outside of the infirmary, like I was getting ready to leave, and this woman, Maddie, said "Please! Don't leave me here!" She just kept screaming it over and over in this shrill scratchy voice. She was ghastly, all gray and white, with hollow eyes. All she had on was like a hospital gown, thing. Her hair was black and though it looked matted and dirty, it was stiff and shiny. I don't know what I'm saying. This probably sounds insane. Next thing I knew I was back in my

10

bed, and I'm not sure if I was still dreaming, but her face was right in front of me and she cried out "Help Me!" I jumped up, wide awake, and screamed so loud it woke Mike up. It's becoming more than I can take. Hope to hear from you soon.

~Hil"

The table had fallen silent, and though there were the usual sounds and conversations around us, it seemed as if we heard nothing. Looking around, I noticed none of my mates were looking up, only staring blankly down at the maps and other papers on the table in front of them. I wanted to say something, but I had no idea of where to begin after reading such a disturbing and desperate email. The muteness of our gathering was becoming more uncomfortable by the second, so much so that I was screaming out in my head, '*SAY SOMETHING!*'.

"But, still..." Katie spoke, and I exhaled loudly, as if I had been holding my breath. "How does she know it's someone named Maddie? I mean, I'm not trying to be difficult, but honestly...how?"

She had a good point, and Theo acknowledged it by looking at her and then me with eyebrows raised. Very animatedly, and clumsily, Jenn plopped her chin down into her hand, her elbow already resting on the tabletop and looked from Katie to me and pushed up her lower lip, crinkling her chin, as if to say 'so....?'

"Hilary can explain better than I can, but she said she has dream visits from her almost every time she goes to the infirmary, and somehow she told her who she was... we'll have to ask her in person, or something." I said, giving them little substance to grasp on to, but they seemed temporarily pacified. At the very least, I felt like I was no longer under pressure to answer the question.

"Okay..." Theo dragged the word out slowly. "Do we know anything other than 'Maddie'? Like, do we know if that's a real person, or anything?"

11

"Hilary did call her Madison once, so I am guessing Maddie is a nickname." I actually was able to give a half-assed answer to that question. As soon as the words left my mouth, Katie began fumbling through her papers. Jenn and Theo soon joined in the action and all three began scanning through the pages, apparently searching for the name Maddie or Madison.

"It's not here." Katie said with disappointment.

"I didn't see anything either." Jenn added.

"True, I didn't find anything either, but it did state clearly that this was an incomplete list and only covered twenty years." Theo had made a statement that was not only true, but also defended the possibility that Hilary knew who was haunting the Infirmary and her dreams. "It's just a feeling, but I think Hilary is right...I think it's Maddie."

As usual, Theo was selling himself short. When I had a feeling, a hunch, or a gut instinct, sometimes I would be right, sometimes not. Theo, on the other hand, had decades and even generations of psychic intuitive history and his 'feelings' were right far more often than wrong. The team felt the same as I did, and gave Hilary and Theo the benefit of the doubt. We decided to stick with searching for a connection between the Infirmary, the adjacent poor house, and someone named Maddie or Madison.

We had only scratched the surface, but at least we had a direction to begin investigating and researching. Often we investigate a haunting without a single shred of evidence to explain the who or why. Many times it is only a vague series of unexplained occurrences that lead someone to believe they have a paranormal situation, while other cases have sightings of apparitions, shadow people, and other supernatural events that substantiate a haunting. Most often these cases have no historical proof of any tragedy or name any particular person of interest that may be trapped spiritually causing the haunting. With this case, we had both. There were numerous tragedies and deaths that were clearly documented in public records. We also had a name, and though it wasn't much to go on, it was more than we were used to.

The conversation turned from the new case, to current events, our personal lives, and eventually to Katie's newborn. He was just over a month old, and my mind drifted back through more than a decade of memories of my own son. I smiled.

"You know this is the first time I have been out of the house without him since he was born?" Katie said, thoughtfully.

"...And this is how you spend your first hours of freedom?" Jenn poked at her, having raised three kids of her own.

"Well... I am honored to have a team meeting as the first thing to drag you away from him. I know it isn't easy when they are so young." I spoke from my own memories.

"I agree, it isn't what I expected my first hours away from him to be, but it's not far from home, and I can go anytime I need to..." Katie's eyes looked upward, as if deep in thought, or memory. "I will eventually get a 'girl's night out' or something more adventurous, just not yet."

"Baby steps..." Jenn whispered and smiled. "Baby steps..."

"Exactly... that's the best way to start, and before long, he'll be getting into everything, and coloring on the walls." I teased her, but also interjected a bit of inevitable truth. That boy, like any, would prove to be a handful!

When the coffees where gone, and we'd run out of things to talk about, we all scattered like ashes in the wind, back to our own lives, and awaited the next clues we might receive. I had hoped that Hilary, Jenn and Katie would soon meet and begin delving deeper into the archives of the small town of Bangs, Ohio. I couldn't help but think there must be something more than just a lost soul, wanting peace. Surely, there were many spirits in need of help. Why had one in particular chosen to be so menacing to our friend from the north? I could only speculate all of the possible reasons, and hope that we might be able to answer the question, and to help her find her eternal peace.

Photo by Rick Kueber

CHAPTER 2
A DREAM OF DEATH

More than a week had passed and aside from a few social media and text messages, I hadn't really spoken to Hilary. The only thing that had actually been said about the Infirmary was my suggestion that she contact Jenn and Katie to set a time to Skype and discuss any further discoveries. I laid down to sleep on a Friday night, and tossed sleeplessly for several hours before I was able to attain any type of rest that even resembled sleeping.

Far away, in the next time zone, Hilary had tucked herself into bed while Mike was off working the night shift, as was usual. She had not had as difficult a time falling asleep as I had, though she may have wished she had.

***

It was a warm sunny afternoon as Hilary and Mike wandered the grounds of the Infirmary and the Poorhouse, with map and sharpie in hand searching for the lost pauper's grave yard. Three cemeteries had been mentioned in the writings of various books and papers, but only one was a marked cemetery. One of the remaining two was unmarked, even on the maps Hilary had found. As they searched they crossed off small bits of property on the map: discovery via process of elimination. Hilary's tummy growled angrily at her and she turned to ask Mike where and when he wanted to go for lunch.

"Mike!" she called out, finding that he had unexpectedly gone missing. She spun about in a panic, not finding him, and called out even louder than before, "MIKE!"

Clouds whirled overhead and the sky grew forbiddingly dark in an instant. Hilary's long dark hair blew in the suddenly wild wind, covering her face. She reached up, pulling the strands from her open mouth and called out again, "MIKE!" just as the lightning struck nearby with a thunderous roar. Bewildered, she found herself now, within the walls of the old Infirmary. It had become black as night outside and as cold as a northern Ohio winter, as the pouring rain pelted the imperfect glass of the ancient windows. Breath as white as snow steamed from her mouth as she wrapped her arms tightly around herself, rubbing her upper arms and shoulders. A phantom breeze blew icy across her neck and nipped stingingly at the rims of her ears. She turned to cry out for Mike once again, but her voice was stolen from her and not a sound would come out.

Manifesting through the darkness, the figure of Maddie appeared. Only a shadow of a figure at first, but moment by moment the details grew clearer. Dressed in the plain white hospital gown, stained and soiled like a discarded napkin, her long, thin frame gave it the appearance of being too large and too small at the same time. Her shiny, coal black hair was stringy and unkempt, but unnaturally covered her face from right to left as if it were windblown, yet frozen in time, and unmoving. Behind it, Hilary could see her eyes showing through, glistening black and lifeless. Bits of skin and flesh were missing from her left leg, arm, and side of her face, leaving random, blackish patches on her otherwise blue-gray skin. Her arms began to reach out to Hilary with twitching boney fingers.

"Hel...p meeeee..." the stuttered whisper came from nowhere and everywhere, filling Hilary's ears and mind with a hagridden voice and

16

the painful sensation that can only be equaled to a migraine that came on as fast as a brain-freeze from eating ice cream to fast. The desire to scream out in sheer pain and horror was constant and though the need was ever present, her voice was not. The vision of Maddie began to blur and distort as wisps of smoky fog began to swirl around them both. Hilary felt herself being pulled backward, as the distance grew between them.

"Please..." Maddie's words drug out painfully. "Don't leave me... here."

The frigid night air became sub-zero and Hilary felt as if she would freeze to death in the moments the words were spoken. Suddenly, all went black.

Gasping for breath, Hilary shot upright in her bed. A cold sweat covered her and dampened her night shirt. Her hands rubbed the sweat from her face and her clammy fingers wrenched through her tangled hair. Exaggerated breaths caused her chest to heave until she gained lucidity once again. *'What a freakin nightmare'* she thought to herself. Feeling the fear induced goosebumps, she rubbed her arms slowly. Still shaken from the vivid vision in her dreams, she sat up on the edge of her bed and reached towards the nightstand to get a cigarette in order to calm her nerves. Looking to the window, she heard the call of a screech owl in the tree outside. The moonlight dimmed as if clouds were moving to mask its light.

Hilary strained her eyes, looking out through the window to the trees beyond. Blue glowing eyes met hers, not from the distant tree line, but immediately in front of her. The eyes dimmed and blackened as she found herself face to chilling face with Maddie. The ghastly woman screamed out in a shrill, shrieking vocalization of terror, and was suddenly gone. Hilary held her breath and her hand shook, still reaching toward the pack of smokes on her nightstand.

A voice whispered quietly, desperately, in her ear. "Don't forget me." Hilary spun about on her bed, looking from side to side and behind her. She swiftly grabbed at the lamp on the nightstand and turned it on, proving to herself that she was alone in the room. Seconds passed, but with hands still shaky, she pulled a cigarette out of the pack and fumbled the lighter clumsily. Taking a deep draw on the lit cigarette, she exhaled the smoke with a calming sigh. Legs trembling, she stood and strolled the few short steps to the window, opening it to let the smoke out and the warm fresh night air in.

"Gawd, I've got to tell Rick about this." She said aloud into the night. *'It's 2 a.m.'* she thought *'maybe I should just write it in a text, If I don't, I might forget some of the details.'* Even though she knew she would never forget this night or the dreams and experiences that would be eternally tied to it. The conversation she had in her head rambled in broken thoughts and brilliant memories. *'I can never write this as well as I remember it, or could tell it...'* The frustration and distress began to build. *'SCREW IT! I'll just write it the best I can, and ask him to call me after he reads it.'* ...and so she did.

***

I awoke like clockwork from one of my typical night's sleep. I had gone to bed on Friday night around 11 pm and tossed and turned until I finally fell asleep sometime around 3 am. There were times I felt fortunate to have such an accurate biological clock... and mornings like this when I cursed it for existing at all. I took my phone from the nightstand and unplugged it. The screen lit up and read: '7:00 am- 1 New Message- Hil.' I unlocked the screen and proceeded to dive into the lengthy message from Hilary detailing her nightmare. I read over it a few times to allow it to sink in as I cleared the cobwebs from my waking mind. I had decided to respond to the text, knowing that my friend may not be awake this early on a Saturday morning. My reply simply read, "Call me when you are up and available."

While I waited to hear from Hilary, I drug myself to the kitchen and began brewing a strong pot of coffee. My mind revisited the story I had read of Hilary's nightmare and I began to visualize what she must have dreamt. I kept having a reoccurring vision of the matted black hair and compelling, empty eyes... a distorted, vague yet gruesome face. Between the flashes of this horrific face, I had imagined how terrifying it must have been for Hilary to see or feel others tearing the skin off of her body. Could there have been some other reason for her night terror, such as having watched some horror film? It was difficult to imagine why anyone would be ripping the skin off of another person, and how demented a person would have to be to do such a thing. The aroma of strong Colombian coffee pulled me back to reality and I doctored up a large mug full of sugar, French vanilla creamer and a splash of very strong coffee. "Mmmm..." I moaned aloud. The warm java began to awaken every fiber of my being, from the inside out. I topped off my mug and carried it to the living room where I settled into my comfy couch and pressed the tv power button on the remote control.

Surfing through the channels, I settled on an 80's film I had seen a dozen times or more, yet I still found enjoyment in watching it and revisiting my youth. Just as I was becoming emotionally involved in the movie, my phone dinged. It was a text from Hilary asking if I could talk via Skype, and I quickly answered yes. I removed myself to the office where my computer screen was already lit up with an incoming video call.

"Hey, Hilary!" I answered.

"Hey..." She replied, sounding less than enthusiastic. We went through all of the cordial greetings and how-have-you-beens and swiftly moved into the meat of the conversation. Hilary went into every detail she could remember. When she paused, I would quiz her and pry forgotten bits and pieces of her dreams from the deep recesses of her memory, and after another line or two of her dream story, I would dissect it asking every possible question about the most infinitesimal detail.

"Do you remember about having your skin torn off?..." I could see that she did by the displeasure of her facial expression. "Was it like being skinned...like all in one piece, or were they tearing bits off, you know, like using their finger nails... or..." I was making myself feel a bit squeamish and couldn't imagine what she must be thinking.

"I don't know how to explain it, really. I could sense a couple of people near me...like overpowering people... and I couldn't move a muscle." Her face contorted with discomfort as she recalled the nightmare. "Have you ever been waxed?"

"Um..." I nearly burst out with laughter, but managed to contain myself. "You mean, like, hair removal...waxing?... No, I haven't."

Hilary rolled her eyes. "I know, dumb question...but you never know. Working in a spa, it's the only thing I can it relate it to. It was like having half of my body waxed, or maybe like fly paper or something." She sighed deeply. "I swear, I'm not crazy, and I know it probably sounds like I am."

"I've had some pretty insanely vivid dreams or visions of my own, so...no, I don't think you're crazy." I smiled at her to comfort her distress. "Your imagery is very good. I can sort of picture it in my head, so you have done well in your description."

We continued on going over every second of the dream from start to finish and then went through it, and all of the uncovered details, again. The conversation was winding down when she offered up a bit of hopeful information.

"I'm meeting with the Bangs Local Historian to go through some of the Infirmary documents that aren't readily available to the general public, so hopefully I can send you some stuff soon." She boasted.

"Looking forward to it! Can you email anything you find to me?" My voice bubbled over with anticipation.

"Yeah. I can scan it in and send it to you." Hilary confirmed my request.

I began to feel more optimistic about the Infirmary case. We may finally be able to make some headway, but my hopes did not translate to the reality that came into fruition. Our liaison for the infirmary case, my dear friend Hilary, became sick. One ailment after another began to pummel her just when she was about to uncover some previously hidden information that could prove vital to our research. Hilary, her husband Mike, and I stayed in sporadic contact. I would text or call to see how she was doing, and more often than not, I was given information on some new medical issues that had arisen. One particular phone call had me frightened, as Hilary was actually scared for her life, and cried to me over the phone, asking why this had all happened to her and what she had done to deserve this. I had no answers, though I had to fight back the fear that it was somehow related to the haunting and negative energy that surrounded the Infirmary, and the spirits that refused to leave her in peace. The illnesses and medical disorders had a definitive reason, a reason none of us would have imagined, but that is another book in itself. All we could do was to bide our time, say our prayers and hope for Hilary's full recovery. 'Time is relative' is a vague statement and only when confronted with how intricate that can be, does one truly begin to understand the concept. The updates came and went painfully slowly, and were interjected throughout the spring time which, in itself, seemed to fly by like dotted lines on the interstate.

***

While Hilary began to recover her health slowly, she received a large manila envelope in the mail with no return address. There was a subliminal concern that troubled her. Her name and address were hand written and she wondered who would send something to her with the need for anonymity. It hadn't come certified, so she felt confident that it wasn't any legal documents, a subpoena, or something of that nature. Still, she felt hesitant to open it, as if it were exuding some bad energy or held some bad news or threatening letter or photos. She sat the burdensome envelope down on the coffee table as she poured a glass of wine. Hilary took her glass and made herself comfortable on the couch, staring at the daunting package. A flood of possibilities ran through her mind like a raging river filled with turmoil and despair.

'What the hell am I so worried about?' she thought, 'What's the worst it could be...notice of termination? No, that would have come certified mail...hate mail from an ex? But why would they send it in an envelope this big? Somebody have incriminating photos of me or Mike's past, or worse, present? God, I hope not!' Her imagination and worry were doing a great job of unraveling her sanity. Her last thought was, 'Uni-bomber?' and that made her giggle, just a little. Hilary was filling her glass for the third time when she came to a conclusion: If this was sent to me, and I was the one who actually brought in the mail, then I must be meant to open it and receive whatever it holds.

She downed the last half of her glass in one drink, popped the glass down on the table with a little extra exertion. Without another moment's hesitation, she snatched up the ominous delivery and ran her finger vigorously under the seal to open it.

"Ow! Shit!" She exclaimed, paper-cutting her index finger. "Well, if this isn't an omen..." She spoke out to the empty house and then reprimanded herself for talking to herself. "You *are* going nuts girl." She left the opened envelope on the table while she scurried to the bathroom to wash and bandage the rather large paper cut. When she returned she noticed the random few crimson drops in sharp contrast to the pale manila of the envelope and it caused her to pause once again, long enough to pour one more glass of wine and take another sip before returning to the portentous task at hand. She pulled the papers out of the envelope and began reading them. She felt relieved and uneasy all at the same time. *'Aw, hell! I've gotta send this to Rick.'* She quickly scanned the pages into a computer file and sent them in an email.

It was evening when I sat down in front of my computer with a microwaved carton of chicken fried rice. I scanned through the subject line of a dozen or more new emails, when one caught my eye. The sender: Hilary, the subject line: Holy FUCK. Hilary had always had a sailor's vocabulary, and her filter had long been discarded. I merely smiled and shook my head when I saw it, but I knew it must hold some importance, so I chose to open it first. Truth is, it ended up being the only email I would read that night, and I read it over and over again.

Rick,

I got this in the mail with no return address and a letter that just said:

Don't publicize this, please. I will contact you soon. I have more information and will talk to you in person when I can assure anonymity.

And that's all it said. Call me when you check it out and have time to take it all in.

Hil

I opened the attachments to the email and printed them out before reading much, but I could instantly tell one of them was some sort of recorded document, another was a newspaper page, and the third was the original letter. I looked at the print outs closely. The short, handwritten letter on unlined paper was exquisitely written, near perfect penmanship, and even without lines to follow, a straight edge showed that every letter, every punctuation mark landed perfectly. This was not recklessly sent, but most likely meticulously thought out and sent with intention. The record documented evidence of a horrific tragedy which had understandably been buried and hidden from the infirmary's history. The same event was once chronicled in the local Bang's newspaper and a scan of the original was the last printout that I read. I was flabbergasted at its revelations.

"TRAGEDY STRIKES THE INFIRMARY

October 13, 1887

After two years of confinement in his first floor room, Adam Clayborne, being 46 years of age and an inmate at the Infirmary since its opening, escaped his restraints and murdered three Infirmary residents on various floors at approximately 2 o'clock in the morning, on Wednesday. The guards and attendees were confounded as to how this man escaped and murdered three individuals in such a violent manner without alerting the night staff. Upon reaching the fourth floor unnoticed, Mr. Clayborne rendered the on-duty guard unconscious with a blow to the posterior of the head. Mr. Clayborne then continued in his deliberate path to enter the room next to the attending psychiatrist's quarters and killed another sleeping inmate by strangling him bare-handedly. The Fourth floor guard, having

23

regained his constitution, found the disgruntled inmate attempting to break into the psychiatrist's quarters. The guard, Mr. Alan Potts retrieved his gun from its holster and shot Mr. Clayborne in his right shoulder. The inmate gave chase back into the inmate's quarters where the strangled man lay. The guard was quoted as saying "...he (Clayborne) had a terrifying fire in his eyes and snarled at me. Fearing for his life, and the lives of others at the infirmary, Mr. Potts fired a second shot, contacting Mr. Clayborne in the left chest. In turn, Mr. Clayborne let out a terrible, inhuman shriek and leapt through the closed window glass and met his demise after abruptly striking the ground below."

Adam Clayborne had been institutionalized for being a mute and being frightened and intimidated to be around other people, making him anti-social to the point of doing harm to his own well-being. Though the record and article were valid proof of the occurrences, the most unnerving revelation was the cause for the inmate's barbaric actions. The staff psychiatrist wrote and signed off on the records which stated:

"Mr. Adam Clayborne, being a very timid and isolated man, acted completely out of character when, on Wednesday morning, not having ever had the occasion to leave his own room, cruelly murdered three inmates, and had he been given opportunity, countless others. After much consultation and deliberation with the Scholar Medical Board, it has been determined that Mr. Clayborne must have been possessed by one or more demons, controlling his actions on this particular night to carry out their wishes. A local clergyman, Fr. Gaunt, was called and having been granted permission by the Bishop will arrive to bless the areas with Holy Water and prayer on Saturday afternoon..."

The report continued with no other information that concerned our investigation, other than the particulars of which rooms had been occupied by Mr. Clayborne, the murdered inmates, and the psychiatrist. I was speechless and had to consider all of the potential ramifications this information could have. The mere mention of the word Demonic changed everything. I had to think about the dangerous consequences this could have for Hilary, my team, and me. The results could not only cause grave issues for all of us, but also for our families and close friends. There were moments, numerous moments, when I considered turning all of the evidence back over to Hilary and washing our hands of this case and all of its overwhelming concerns. Snatching up my phone I began to dial... my first instinct was to call Hilary. As soon as I began to punch in her number, I knew what needed to be done first. It was my team... I had started it, but it had grown and transformed many times into what it now was, and would surely transform again throughout its future. The reality became clear to me, it was our team, and decisions that affected it should be made as a team. It was time for coffee...

Through some divine, miraculous intervention, Jennifer called at that moment and asked if I had plans for the evening, saying she and Katie had been talking and since we hadn't had a meeting in a while, they wanted to just 'hang out' as a team. I couldn't have been happier to meet up. After a long refreshing and rejuvenating, hot shower, I stood in front of the steam covered mirror, wrapped in a towel and my mind wandered. I ran my hand across the mirror, revealing the haggard face that stared back at me. There was a familiarity in this stranger's face. It was older and thinning hair was becoming flecked with silver and the stress of the past few years were written in lines that had not been there a short time ago. As I gazed deep into the sadness of the dark brown eyes in the reflection, it occurred to me that my soul had aged far more than my face. I hadn't told the team that there was any news from the infirmary, and I struggled with whether or not to divulge the information tonight, or 'just hang out' as it had been put to me. It sounded wonderful to meet with my team...my friends...with no other purpose other than to spend an evening together and have a good time. While I contemplated these things, I began to get dressed. I constantly checked the time, until I could wait no longer, I grabbed up the latest correspondence from Hilary, tossed it into the passenger seat and started up the old convertible. I put the top down and as I began to drive off, a breeze blew in and scattered the papers. Throwing the car into park, I frantically gathered up the pages and folded then up small enough to shove the bulky mess into my front pocket.

Sitting in the parking lot of Banes and Noble, I looked around to see Jenn's black Camry already parked and empty. Somehow, I felt a sense of awkward relief to not be the first to arrive. I entered the bookstore and found my way to the Starbuck's coffee shop nestled in the front corner. Stepping into the line, I looked over the busy cafe and located a corner booth where Theo, Jenn and Katie were already seated and chatting over steaming caffeinated goodness. I approached them with my delectable latte in hand and stood at the end of the booth table, towering over them. Looking from one to another, the clamber of their chit-chat dulled and slowly fell silent. All at once their faces grew somber and all eyes turned to me, awaiting some sobering news... I had them right where I wanted them, and so I began.

"Dearly beloved, we are gathered here today to join this man," I gestured to myself. "and this latte... in holy, heavenly, though short lived bliss." Rousing laughter ensued, and I felt suddenly younger than I had less than an hour ago.

"What the hell was that all about?" Jennifer managed to get out through her giggles.

"Yeah!" Katie spouted. "Here, I thought you were about to tell us the Ohio gig was canceled or worse..." Theo only grinned silently, but his grin faded as I sat down across from him. Somehow, he knew... he always had a way of knowing.

"It is worse, isn't it?" He said, in a quiet and reserved tone.

"We'll get to that soon enough, but for now, how is everybody? It seems like forever since we met last." I tried to divert the topic, unsuccessfully, I might add.

"We're all good...is this 'soon enough' for ya... cause you can bet your ass, it's soon enough for us." Jenn said bluntly, but though her words were harsh and to the point, I could sense there was more concern and care in her intent than her words were revealing.

"Okay... I get it." I said, losing my smile and drawing the wadded mess of papers out of my pocket. I tossed them on the table in the midst

26

of everyone and they laid there like they were plague ridden. Everyone stared, but no one would dare touch them.

"What's this?" Theo asked, not allowing me to passively give them the information.

"It's some stuff Hil sent me. Make of it what you will, but I want you all to know, if you don't want to stay involved with this case, I completely understand." I waited for someone to unfold the papers. Much to my surprise, Katie reached for them first and slowly unfolded them, laying them flat on the table and pressing and sliding her hand across them to smooth out the wrinkles and creases. Theo and Jenn looked at the papers in front of Katie and tried to make sense of any words they could read from their angle. As Katie finished reading each page she passed them to Theo, who in turn passed them to Jenn. The table was silent within its own bubble of reality while the seemingly carefree world around us went gallivanting about its own boisterous business.

"Well..." Jenn broke the spell of silence. "That sure adds a whole new level of creepiness to the Infirmary investigation."

"And danger..." I added. "If anyone wants out, now's the time, and I think I know us all well enough to say that you won't be judged, and it won't affect your standing with the team."

"Why?" I was shocked to hear Katie's response, though I wasn't sure what she meant. I just looked at her, non-verbally asking her for more. "Why is 'now the time'?" She sipped her drink, while everyone's attention turned to her. "I mean, why can't we back out at any time? Like...what if I want to keep helping with the research and decide later if I want out of the actual trip to the Infirmary?" She had me.

"I just thought when you all read that this may be demonic, that you might want out...especially considering *your* little guy." I nodded toward Katie. "This is a tricky place to be, as a team leader... this is both a team and an individual decision. Do we proceed as a team, partial team, or not at all. There are probably others who are better suited to deal with

27

this kind of a haunting." I left it at that for them to think about.

"You have a..." Theo started but was cut off by Katie who was more vocal than usual.

"Why?!?" She nearly shouted, causing a few random onlookers and making us shrink in our seats just a bit. "I'm pretty proud of us. We've been through a lot just in the last year and a half alone... and if you are insinuating that anybody else could care any more than we do, then I think you're wrong."

I found myself speechless once again. Katie was rarely so outspoken as she was today, but her statements, though strongly stated, made me beam with pride. I opened my mouth to try to say something, anything...but was saved by Theo who spoke up first.

"As I was about to say..." He began, smiling to Katie. "You have a good point, but just because something has been labeled as 'demonic' doesn't mean that it is. There are plenty of negative entities and spirits that are even more evil in death than they were in life. I can't explain why a timid man would suddenly become a violent mass murderer, but diagnoses in the 1800's were not nearly as accurate as they are today, and we don't really know what this person had been through, or why he seemed to target certain people for his brutal executions...but we do know that we have faced a demonic presence before, and we have managed to help many souls, living and passed. I think we should see this through, no matter how long it takes, no matter who can, or can't...who will or won't help." He sat back, having said his piece.

Jenn held her hand up. "I'm good." She said, and I thought that was all I was going to get from her. "As long as I have my sage and my prayers, I'm all in. I agree with Katie. I think I'll know before I get in to deep, and if we decide it's too much, we'll decide when that time comes, but I'll be damned if I'm going to give up before then... and don't expect me to give up, even then."

"Okay. I get it." I looked each one of them in the eyes and smiled. I was actually fighting back the emotions as my eyes began to water.

Quickly, I grabbed my latte and took a big drink. "Damn that's hot!" I fanned at my mouth as my watery eyes rolled a tear or two out onto my cheeks. I could feel their empathy, and thought they would not put me on the spot. What was I thinking?

"Nice try E.V.Prick!" Jenn laughed out. "You aren't fooling anyone. My coffee's been cold for ten minutes." She grinned. "But it's okay, I..." I could see the depth of her emotion stealing the words from her, but her feelings could not be stifled and came across loud and clear.

We wrapped up what was intended to be a casual meeting as casually as we could, discussing topics such as our kids, work, and other facets of our daily lives. We might have stayed longer if we had known how long it would be before we would meet again. As intuitive as some of our team was, none of us anticipated such lengthy separation.

Photo by Grace Kirsch

Chapter 3
A Dashing Young Woman

As time passed, I began to lose hope, not hope of aiding Hilary and the souls in need at the Infirmary, but hope that I would once again find a love who would be my twin flame, my soul-mate, and would love me as much as I did her for the rest of our lives. I had remained a single dad, and though I pined for the love of a woman who was the most amazing friend a person could wish for, those dreams and desires remained unattained. My love was much like the flowers potted on my front porch: they were noticed, but unattended and though they had no greater desire than to flourish and receive a drenching down pouring of rain from the heavens, they grew weaker as time passed and their needs, and mine, remained unquenched and withered.

It was without intention, but the weeks passed all too quickly. The days grew warmer and longer, spring became summer, and Katie's tiny infant was becoming a cotton topped boy. Somehow, though we all remained in contact with each other and Hilary, the summer solstice came and went. The heat of June mid-days turned into sultry July mornings. The 4th of July holiday passed us like it had everyone else and my son's birthday, which was only one short week away, was rapidly approaching and soon after that school would begin again...and still, we had not made it to the infirmary as we had planned.

It was on a scorching July afternoon, a Saturday, when we finally met at the office as a team and I placed a skype call to Hilary, as had been previously planned. Surprisingly, Jenn had arrived first and I received her calling card greeting.

"Hey there, E.V.Prick! How ya been?" accompanied by the all too predictable hug.

"Not bad, I suppose...all things considered." I answered honestly, though in my head I was thinking things would be better if I didn't feel so lonely and if we had been able to at least have an initial investigation at the infirmary.

"So, what's up with the Infirmary?" Jenn asked bluntly.

"You know...I was just thinking that our last two major cases were wrapped up within a few months of receiving the initial information." I began.

"Yeah..." Jenn said slowly, attempting to draw out the rest of my thoughts.

"...and it's been more than three months since we received the call from Hil, and all we have done is scratched the surface of researching, and haven't even made it up there to investigate yet." I said, disheartened, and drew my mouth up to one side as I finished.

"True..." She couldn't argue the facts, but thought for a moment before saying, "...but you are in construction, and I am in horticulture and landscaping. This is the crazy-busy time of year for us. I can barely find time to shower at the end of the day; much less make a trip to northern Ohio!"

"I know. I know…" I had to agree. I had been incredibly busy.

"Hey now! That wasn't very nice!" Jenn threw her hands on her hips and my eyes widened, wondering what I had said wrong.

"You didn't have to agree with me. I do shower you know…and on a regular basis." She grinned, and I half smiled back at her, wishing my spirits could rise to her level.

It was just then that I noticed Theo pulling into a parking space out front. I opened the sliding glass door to welcome him in when the heat of the day blasted me like opening an oven door. The day was in the upper nineties, but the humidity and 'heat index' made it nearly unbearable. I hadn't planned on leaving the door open long, but just as Theo stepped from his car, Katie pulled in as well, so I stepped out into the heat to greet them and closed the door behind me. We shook hands and said our hellos on the front patio and I slid the glass door open and listened as they both let out a sigh of relief as they entered the cool 72 degree apartment. Jenn greeted them in the same way she had greeted me, with hugs and sarcasm, and we expected no less. A short time later we all shuffled into the spare room that I had set up as our team office. While my three amigos chose their seats next to the makeshift desks, I stood in the doorway.

"Drinks?" One word was all I needed to say.

"Margaritas?" Jenn joked.

"Um…nope… but I have Mt. Dew, Diet Dew, tea, water, or I could make coffee." I felt like an airline steward listing drinks and taking orders.

Jenn stuck her tough out in her usual child-like way and spluffed. "No Dr. Pepper? Ugh! I guess I'll have a Diet Dew."

"Is the tea sweetened?" Theo asked and I nodded with a smile. "Okay. Tea for me, then."

"Water." was Katie's response and did not surprise anyone.

Theo followed me into the Kitchen and I directed him to the

cabinet where I kept the drinking glasses.

"The ice is in the freezer." I added and Theo shot me a sideways glance.

"Thanks... I was about to look in the microwave." In my head I was thinking *smart ass* but I refrained from saying it out loud and causing Theo to possibly drop the glass. Somehow, he knew what I was thinking, and so we both had a good chuckle as I retrieved the pitcher for him. While he poured his glass, I grabbed drinks for the rest of us and then returned to the office. I rolled the only open chair up to my computer and began opening files and printing four copies of each. When the first set had finished printing, I passed them out, keeping one for myself.

"Okay...here's the latest and the greatest information Hilary had dug up from her level-7, top-secret hidden archives that only Nicholas Cage could find." Everyone got the reference and it was greeted with a flurry of smiles and eye rolls and one "Only you Rick." from Jenn.

I already had a chance to read over the documents that I received that day, so while the others looked them over, I contacted Hilary via Skype and had her live on screen by the time everyone had looked over the first document.

"Hey everybody!" Hilary called out and I could see her looking around to see who all was on the other end of the call. Everyone leaned in front of the camera and smiled and waved, or said hello back. "So...what do you think? Have you looked at the stuff I sent yet?"

"I just printed them out and everyone has the first one, you know, the three newspaper clippings about people falling out of the windows." I stated and smiled at the camera. I could sense Hilary's energy. She was both excited to begin revealing the discoveries she had worked so diligently to find, but there was also a more comfortable feeling. There was already a peace that came with her belief that we would finally be able to put this haunting to rest. Perhaps it was the cliched 'calm before the storm'.

December 17, 1886   Martin Davis

Died tragically Friday evening at the age of 63 whilst expectorating out of a fourth floor window. Mr. Davis lost his footings and fell to his demise. Two male attendees witnessed the fall but were not able to secure Mr. Davis. Mr. Davis had been confined as an inmate at the Infirmary after exposure in the Army.

February 4, 1887   Myrtle Louisa Graham

The widow Graham died unexpectedly at the age of 47 when she plummeted to her death. Ms. Graham had been avoiding two Infirmary Attendees when she fell through the window glass of her fourth story room. Ms. Graham had been admitted to the Infirmary after her excessive sexual abuse had been discovered.

November 28, 1887   Clement Butler

Mr. Butler died shortly after an accidental fall from a window in his fourth floor room. Two male attendees had gone to collect Mr. Butler for his weekly bath when they discovered the mishap. Clement Butler passed at the young age of 33 after suffering from epileptic seizures for several years at the Infirmary.

"So...why did they house people with 'mental' issues on the fourth floor?" Jenn queried.

"That does seem like a bad move, and apparently, they kept the windows open, or unlocked, which seems like a really stupid idea for the fourth story of a mental hospital." Theo added in agreement.

"Yeah... you would think they would have bars on the windows after the first one fell, or at least keep them locked." Hilary interjected. "...and did you notice how they all happened in the winter? Who the hell would have the windows open in northern Ohio in the winter? That's just insane!"

"Good point. Being from southern Indiana, I wouldn't have even really made that connection. Sometimes we have 60 degree days in December... not often, but once in a while." I applauded Hilary's observation.

"Anybody notice any other odd coincidences?" Katie said quietly, as if she were hesitant to say anything.

"Like what?" Jenn asked.

"Well, maybe it's nothing, but there were two attendants that saw or found all three of them, and two times it said they were males, aaaand... the woman who fell through the window was 'avoiding' them. First thing that comes to mind is that they were chasing her, or trying to take her someplace she didn't want to go...maybe she was more afraid of them than she was of jumping through the window... or maybe I'm just reading too much into it." Katie looked down at the floor and awaited the critiquing.

"BAM!" Hilary's voice yelled out from the computer speakers. "Show them the other document, Rick!" Excitement was in her voice in anticipation of the reaction they would have to the next uncovered archive. I did not hesitate, and as soon as everyone had their copy, the room fell silent.

What I had handed them was a page from another edition of the 'The Independent Observer', a local newspaper. Even though the team was reading it for themselves, I could not resist reading it aloud to emphasize the key words and phrases.

DASHED TO DEATH

An Inmate from the Local Infirmary

Leaps from a Fourth-Story Window

and is Instantly Killed

Madison Taylor, 25 years of age and unmarried, met with a frightful death at the Local Infirmary Friday evening- January 13, 1888. A former resident of Waverly City, she has been an inmate at the county Infirmary for several years. She has been troubled with a nervous disease that slightly affected her mind, and by reason of her predisposition to run away from the institution, was locked in an apartment on the fourth floor. About 7 o'clock on Saturday evening two men (employees of the Infirmary) having occasion to pass around the building, came upon the inanimate form of a woman on the ground. They reported the matter to Supervisor Ellis and the body was removed to a room on the first floor of the building. It was found to be the Taylor woman and her body was mangled in a most frightful manner. Her hat and shawl were found on the ground near the body. The supposition prevailed that while labouring under mental aberration she had attempted to escape from the institution by leaping from the 4th story window. Her death must have been almost instantaneous, as there was no sign of disturbance to the snow covered ground around the body.

"Holy crap! Madison Taylor... is that our Maddie?" Katie exclaimed nearly jumping from her seat.

"I think so!" Hilary yelled through the computer speakers with enthusiasm while I looked at my team with a devilish grin on my face.

"Time to get your butts to work girls!" I added with a cagey tone. "You've got a name to start diggin' up."

"Can we start now?" Jenn said excitedly. "I wanna start now!" A toothy grin grew on her face.

"I don't see why not." I answered her, but noticed Theo rubbing

37

his forehead with eyes closed.

"You won't find her..." He said as if he was in a daze. "I don't know what that means, but I just know you won't find her."

"We're still going to look, Theo. You could be wrong, you know?" Katie seemed hurt by his words. "This is the best lead we've had yet." No one argued, but Jenn perked up as if she had been shocked by one of those old-time gag 'joy-buzzers' that would pass a jolt to a hand shake recipient.

"Katie!!" She yelled out. "We almost forgot to tell Rick about Mr. Clayborne."

"Oh yeah... well, there isn't a lot to tell, but go ahead." Katie said honestly and they both immediately gained the undivided attention of Hilary, Theo, and me.

Jenn proceeded to open her email on one of the desktop computers. "I sent the info to myself in an email so I could access it anywhere... I always do." It took her a few minutes to find and open the email and its attached files, but once she did, she began to summarize the life of our 'demonic killer'.

"We could only follow him back a few years before the infirmary where he had spent all of his time in psychiatric care and the records all say the same thing as the report...He was a timid man who never spoke a word and was terribly withdrawn from society. We did find another man by the same name and almost identical age who was a soldier with the Confederate Army of Northern Virginia, under General Robert E. Lee. He was one of several troops who joined Beauregard and had a victory in the battle that took the Charleston Federal Fort. Other than that he had a pretty normal life as far as we can tell. Both parents survived through most of his life, he had one sister named Elizabeth but there is no record of her death. This Mr. Adam Clayborne was sent to West Virginia with an entire battalion of men. No one knows exactly what happened, but the entire encampment was slaughtered without a single shot being fired. The most mysterious thing about his history is that he was not among the casualties, and no one knew what ever became of him...unless we just figured it out." She paused.

"If he witnessed the massacre, it could explain his conditions... maybe that's why he was so withdrawn." I offered up one possibility.

"And I've heard of people being 'mute' after witnessing a horrific tragedy. Sort of a Post-Traumatic-Stress-Disorder, thing." Theo added.

"That's kinda what we thought too." Katie chimed in. "There is no direct proof, but me and Jenn really think this is our guy...and while it doesn't necessarily explain why he would suddenly snap, it's the closest match we could find."

"It may not be rock solid evidence, but if we assume this is the same guy, we can also make the assumption that he could have taken all of that fear and negative energy with him to the Infirmary. That is, if I can make a third assumption? If he witnessed the massacre and escaped, he could have taken those energies with him." I was tongue tied and confused over my own words, though in my head the thoughts and ideas were crystal clear. "Did any of that crap I said make any sense to anybody?"

"It made sense to me. If this is our Adam, and he saw the massacre, he could have left the scene with an attachment...he could have even had the spirits of some, or hypothetically even all, of the soldiers follow him where ever he went." Theo had made a good point and clarified what I was trying to say.

"Well then..." Jenn sighed. "I think everybody knows what everybody else knows now, right?" She looked directly at me.

"That's everything I know of." I said honestly. "I'll let you know as soon as I have anything else, and if you find anything out about our Madison Taylor, give me a call, or email or something."

"We definitely will." Katie said. I could feel the enthusiasm in her voice, despite Theo's remarks.

***

Again, time flew by. I had held a meager, yet festive birthday party for my son (who now lived with me), with a few relatives and friends. Soon after, I found myself dragging him through the aisles at the local department store for school supplies and uniforms and the most expensive thing on the 'back to school' list: new shoes. Daniel wasn't picky about much of anything, and made my life easy that way... what he was very particular about was shoes. He wanted the top of the line Nikes, only a few different styles that he would settle for. As difficult as it was to spend as much on his shoes as I had been accustomed to spending on my wardrobe for an entire year or more, I gritted my teeth, smiled and paid the piper. There were times in my youth that I knew quite well what it was like to not have the right shoes and I knew that kids, for whatever reason, judged their peers according to that and could be extremely cruel.

School had been in session for more than a month when my birthday came and went with nothing more than a happy birthday call from my dad. I didn't need much, but I was hoping for a homemade card from my son, or some acknowledgment, but at his age, if no one reminded him, he wouldn't remember. I didn't hold it against him, and never said anything to him about it. Hilary, the team, and I tried and failed on several occasions to plan a trip to investigate the Infirmary. There were always too many conflicts, and so it was that with Halloween rapidly approaching, Hilary and I set a date, and if the rest of the team couldn't make it, at least the actual investigation would have begun. I hoped with all of my heart that everyone could be there. The location was massive, the tragedies were inconceivable, and I needed the expertise of everyone on my team.

We set the investigation for the first Saturday in November. Hilary had warned us that if we waited too long, it would become bitterly cold and wouldn't warm up until May. I spoke individually with the trio of

40

teammates and, much to my surprise, all were willing and able to take the weekend to travel to Northern Ohio. I couldn't have been happier. I planned the trip, budgeted enough money to eat and pay for gas, made arrangements for my son to stay with his friend that weekend, and had checked over the gadgets and gear numerous times to make sure everything was in working order and there was a copious amount of extra batteries on hand. The plan was to leave early on Saturday morning and arrive in time to tour the Infirmary and surrounding property in the daylight.

I had been in working in Louisville on Friday, and as I was heading home at the end of the day I received a text from Jennifer. I simply read, "Call me, please" but my heart sank. I quickly sent the call and waited for her to answer.

"Hey Rick." She said with no levity in her voice.

"Hey Jenn, what's going on?" I was afraid she was going to bail out on the trip, but that wasn't like Jenn at all. She had never missed an investigation.

"Don't say anything to anyone..." She took a deep breath and her voice cracked. "I haven't even told Alan yet." I could hear her beginning to cry softly.

"It's okay...you can talk to me. I've always been here for you, and you know I always will be." I had wished we were having this conversation in person, but I was two hours away.

"Well, you know I went for my 6 month checkup last week, right?" We had discussed it when planning the trip to Ohio. "It's back..." She broke down right there on the phone and all I wanted to do was hug her, but I couldn't. "Why did it come back?"

Jenn had been a cancer survivor and her lymphoma had been in remission. She had been cancer free for years. Her oncologist still required her to have semi-annual checkups, which were always good, and gave us another reason to celebrate when she would receive her report. It was not the case this time. Jenn was utterly distraught and with good reason. The chemo was horrific and of course, it was impossible to not imagine the 'worst case scenario'.

"It's going to be okay Jenn." I made a crappy attempt, with the best of intentions, to comfort her. "You are the toughest person I know, and that's saying a lot. You've beaten this thing before, and as much as it may suck... you're going to beat it again. I just know you will."

"How am I going to tell my kids... how am I going to tell Alan?" She sniffled. "I really just wanted to call to tell you I can't go to Ohio right now..." Her voice trailed off as she thought about what the coming weeks and months might have in store for her. "I haven't told Katie or Theo either, so don't say anything yet, please... I have to go back and see my oncologist next week and have even more tests done. I'll probably let everyone know when I get the test results back and have a better idea of what I'm going to be up against."

"Okay. Be sure to let me know what the doc says...and of course, I won't say a word to anyone. It's not my place to do that." I didn't know what else to say, and I thought the less I say, the better, at least right now.

I hoped she wasn't able to pick up on exactly how frightened I was for her, and how unsure I was of my 'so called' encouraging words. Jenn was the reason EVP became a team... she was the second, only to me. From the beginning, she had been there. It was inconceivable that EVP could exist without her... in fact, the team had become such a family, I could not fathom EVP without all four of us. We had been through so many life changing events together, we had a bond that surpassed friendship, and at times, even some family.

***

The radio played quietly in the background but I paid it no attention. My thoughts were consumed by the news Jenn had just delivered. We had celebrated every good check-up and clean bill of health, like a new birthday, but suddenly all the years of celebrating meant nothing. The drive home seemed never-ending, and I longed for some distraction. Almost as the very thought crossed my mind, my phone rang. I fumbled to pull my phone from my pocket again as I sped down the interstate between Louisville and Evansville. I glanced at the screen before answering -Katie.

"Hey Katie!" I put on a brave face and pretended all was okay. "Are you ready for the next grand adventure?"

"That's why I called..." Her tone was unmistakable. Something was wrong... 'Geez!' I thought. Something else was wrong. "Both of my men have the flu, and I can't leave them here alone. I'm going to have to cancel out on this trip."

"It's okay." I lied. "I'm sure we'll have to make a few visits to the Infirmary, so this trip is just an initial investigation. The next visit will probably be the better investigation anyway."

"I just hate it though! I've been looking forward to this ever since we first got the request... and that's been months!" There was real distress in Katie's voice. It was as if she had just been told that her seven day cruise to the Mediterranean had been canceled. I heard her spluff quietly.

"Honestly Katie, it's no big deal, Jenn can't go either. We will schedule another trip as soon as possible." As true as that statement may have been, I knew it would be months before we would be able to return due to the harsh Northern Ohio winter that was so rapidly approaching, and the holiday gatherings and events that would fill the next few weeks. Truthfully, I worried that Jenn might never get to go to the Infirmary with us. Our conversation ended with me telling Katie to take care of her men, and assuring her that we would let her know every detail as soon as we returned.

The team was now split in half and it felt odd traveling to a new and distant haunted location without the girls. Our weekend investigation had just become exponentially more difficult. Beep-beep... Beep-beep... My phone, still in my hand, abruptly rang again.

"Hey Hilary." My voice was less than monotone. I knew this would be the call that would cancel the investigation, possibly until spring.

"Hey Rick... everything alright?" She asked with a genuinely concerned tone.

"Katie and Jenn both just canceled out on the investigation this weekend... I figured you were calling to do the same." I, most likely, sounded like a child who had just been told his puppy ran away.

"HELL-TO-THE-NO! I mean... sucks that they can't come, but you'd better get your ass up here tomorrow! I have everything worked out, and I can't take much more of Maddie. I seriously have not had a good night's sleep in months." Hilary had a way of making me laugh at even the most terrifying thing.

"Well, thank God!" Even if Theo skips out, I promise I'll be there. I've been planning on this trip for what seems like an eternity!" In spite of the recent phone calls, I began to feel much better, more optimistic... Perhaps it was just a coincidence that both Katie and Jenn weren't able to make it, and not some supernatural force working against us.

"So, what time do you think you'll be here tomorrow?" Hilary

44

asked.

"Not sure. I'll call Theo when I get off the phone and let you know." I had already planned to call Theo, just to make sure he was still going.

"You can just call me when you hit the road, or when you get close if you want. That will give me an idea of when you'll get here and give me plenty of time to do anything I need to get done." Hilary was right. It was nearly a seven hour drive and that was not counting any stops for food or gas.

"Okay, cool. I'll call you in the morning." I replied, lightheartedly.

"Alrighty... talk to you then." The call ended with a beep as she hung up. I was nearing Evansville and decided that I may as well make the last phone call while I was still on the road.

"Hey..." Theo said very calmly and slowly, as if I had awakened him.

"Hey Theo... just checking to see if you were still up for the trip to the Infirmary tomorrow." I nervously awaited his answer.

"Most definitely!" His voice perked up. "I thought maybe you were calling to cancel out. I just had this bad feeling about the trip."

"Nope... I'm still going, good Lord willing. Katie and Jenn both are unable to go, but I just spoke to Hilary and everything is still a 'go' for us." I was relieved that I would not be making this long journey into the unknown alone.

"Oh, well... cool, I guess. Hope everything's alright with the girls." Theo said, as if he knew everything was far from 'alright'. "So what time do you want to head out in the morning?"

"The earlier, the better. What time works for you?" I tossed the

45

question back to him.

"Ten?" He asked.

"Sure, ten is fine. That should get us there while it's still daylight. I really want to check out the place before it gets dark." I had hoped to leave earlier, but I was content with leaving at ten in the morning.

"True..." He agreed. "It is starting to get dark pretty early now. Ten should give us a few hours before the sun goes down."

The plans were set, I had taken my son to spend the weekend with his friend, and I had gone through the equipment cases twice to make sure everything was packed and my OCD was satisfied. It was time for bed, and I was ready for an early night. The drive was going to be long, and the evening and night of investigating was going to be even longer. I needed sleep, and I was anxious to get as much as I could before heading out in the morning. I made a mixed drink of Crown & Coke as a nightcap (which I never do at home and alone) and prepared for bed. Lights were out, and the fan was on high as I crawled into bed and pulled the covers over me. I fell asleep within the hour, which is relatively quick for me, but my sleep was far from peaceful, as dream visitors came to fill my sleep with disturbing visions.

I found myself wandering through a forest under the cover of darkness, not knowing how I came to be there, or where *there* even was. The sounds of cicadas filled the air, accompanied by the episodic hoot of a distant owl. I was moving forward with a purpose, though I had no idea of what that purpose was. I crested the top of a pine covered spoil bank and quickly spied a small fire in the distance and began to hear the muffled canter of several men. Cautiously, I approached. I stopped about thirty yards short of where this large group had made camp and soon realized they were all dressed in confederate uniforms. The fire rapidly dwindled to glowing embers and then darkened to only a few thin

46

ribbons of smoke that could be seen in the dim light of the nearly full moon, and the men moved in swift and stuttered movements, as if everything were moving in fast forward.

There seemed to be no sense of time as a few moments passed, yet with the movement of the moon, I knew it had been hours. Two men appeared within the encampment and began to speak in hushed tones, but were as clear to me as if I were standing right next to them.

"We've seen plenty of things that were purely hell on earth, and this forest is as peaceful as I could imagine..." The first man began to speak. "...but to me, this place is as eerie as I've ever seen."

"There is truth to what you say Adam. I've never cared for West Virginia anyways, but this place just ain't right." Agreed the second soldier. "I've been uncomfortable since we started setting up camp. Somethin's just not right here. I can't sleep. I keep hearing whispers, and somethin's watchin' us... it's out there somewheres... can you feel it too?"

"Yes, Andrew, I can feel it. There's evil in these woods, and we ain't welcome." Adam looked around and I felt as if he would look straight at me, but his gaze passed over me as if I did not even exist. "I'm goin' out to scout out a perimeter... make sure there ain't no yanks or injuns out there ready to ambush us."

"Alright Adam. Just be sure to signal if I need to wake the rest of the fellas." Andrew said, more than satisfied to stay behind and not venture out into the unknown.

Adam loaded his rifle, slid his boots on and quietly sneaked away into the night. I stood frozen in my place, unable to move as he slowly passed by me scanning every inch of the surroundings for unwelcomed visitors. When he had disappeared over the bank to the other side and was completely out of sight, my attention was once again drawn back to the camp. The moonlight had grown brighter as a fog rolled in, but this was no ordinary fog bank. There was no billowing, wispy, white mist, instead, the fog was as black as pitch and obscured the ground and all it covered from sight. Soon the camp was engulfed in the ebony clouds and the shrill screams began. Adam rushed past me toward the camp so swiftly I could feel the wind of his movement, but stopped short, about half way between where I stood and where the encampment was. He was petrified with terror as he watched the soldiers run shrieking in pain from their tents.

The black mists rolled and curled up the legs of the men as they attempted to run, and failed. The sounds of their deaths mortified me and I could not imagine anything that could cause so much torment and pain... not even the memory of my dream of burning to death as little Ashley did. The mist crawled up each man until it had covered them completely like a growing, living thing, as toxic and deadly as sulfuric acid. As the cries of despair diminished and eventually ended altogether, the dark mist began to become concentrated in the center of the camp and took form. I saw it there in the moonlight, a hulking figure, not completely human, not completely demonic. It turned toward me and I saw the light blue glow of its eyes as they focused on young Adam. The beast raised its arms causing the campfire to reignite and suddenly, it let out the most heinous laughter, and as it did, the flames which had grown incredibly tall instantaneously froze solid and then exploded with a roar. Adam fell directly on his back as this hellish creature spread its hidden wings and shot into the sky. Adam had lost control of his bodily functions for a brief moment, but then scrambled to his feet and flew past me moaning with fright. His speed only increased with every step until I could no longer see him.

Time sped up again until the dawn began to break through the trees and I could see the bodies of the men strewn about the camp, their flesh desiccated, seemingly drained of life and fluid. I stared longer than I wanted to at the mummified remains that lay still in their uniforms. Many of the men were still barefoot, having been awakened from a deep sleep by what may as well have been the devil himself. The early morning mists began to thicken until it could barely see the forest that surrounded me.

BEEP- BEEP- BEEP! I awoke to my alarm and wiped the cold sweat from my brow. The day I had been waiting for had come, and I was glad to not be going to West Virginia on this particular day. After the vivid dream I had awakened from, I had no trouble literally jumping out of bed and straight into the shower. A half a pot of coffee later, I was shaved, dressed, packed up and awaiting Theo's arrival.

I loaded my things into Theo's silver-blue Subaru, climbed inside and began a road trip that would be just as long as our trips to the Helmach Farm in West Virginia. We made our stops for gas, breakfast, and eventually lunch along the way. Throughout the trip we held conversations on numerous topics, but we frequently came back to our anticipations of what amazing experiences the Infirmary may hold for us. When we had exited the interstates and found ourselves on winding two-lane highways and country backroads, the feeling in the air took a chilling turn. Perhaps it was our own excitement that we could not contain, but as we drew near to Mike and Hilary's home, and closer to the Infirmary, there was a growing energy in the air.

"Can you feel it?" I asked Theo.

"Oh yeah... you can too, huh?" He answered back, keeping his eyes on the road ahead.

"Look!" I called out and pointed to the clear blue sky. "Pull over!"

"What?!?" Theo yelled back as he skidded the car off to the shoulder of the road. I leapt from the car quickly followed by my

49

teammate and friend. Across the road from where we stood was a flowing waterway and a barren, leafless tree line. I raised my hand to shield my eyes from the glaring sun and we watched as a bald eagle soared and circled overhead until it dove toward the water, snatching up its dinner and then landing high in an empty treetop. I pulled out my phone to snap a photo.

"Check it out." Theo said pointing down the road a hundred feet or so. A green road side sign marked the name of the water and the irony was uncanny.

"Mad River..." I smiled as the words left my lips. "Seems fitting, eh?"

"Very... and seeing the eagle is a very good sign. The spirit symbol of the bald eagle tells us to be on point, be courageous and push our limits. Reach higher, look at things from a higher point of view and be prepared to fly." Theo paused

"Courageous, huh?" I chuckled.

"That's all you picked up on?" Theo joked.

We watched until the eagle took flight again and then disappeared into the distant horizon. We climbed back into the car and zipped down the road with the cool autumn breeze stabbing in through the inch of open window on either side of the car. I pulled my phone out to call Hilary and after a very short conversation we had plans to meet at Hilary and Mike's home to await Mike's return. Once we arrived at the beautiful two story rural home, we were greeted by our friend. We sat in a room just off of the kitchen and burned sage in preparation of the night ahead.

Mike arrived later than expected and the sun was setting on our day. The hopes of familiarizing and searching the Infirmary in the daylight was no longer a possibility. We transferred our equipment into their quad-cab truck and headed out for an unknown that we had long anticipated.

Photo by Rick Kueber

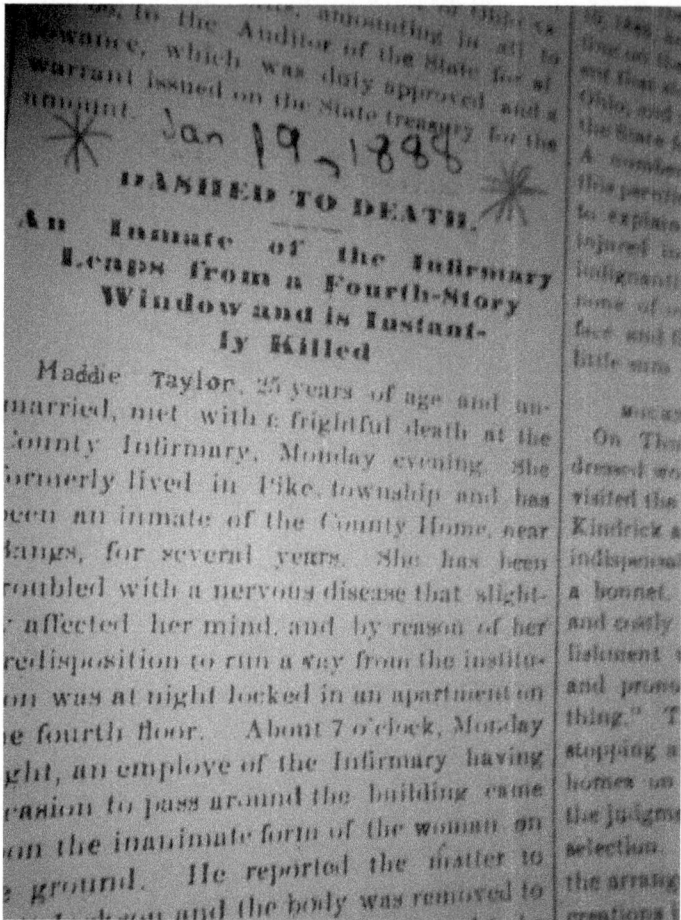

Photo by Rick Kueber

Chapter 4
AND SO, IT BEGINS

It was a chilling night as the quad-cab truck turned off of the main street and onto a narrow, two-lane, country backroad. The clouds were heavy in the blackened and starless sky. Mike drove with Hilary in the front passenger seat. Theo sat behind Mike, meditating as the miles passed and I sat to his right staring out of the window into the barren, lifeless fields as they blurred by in the darkness. The truck slowed as we made yet another turn and remained at an idle pace with the tires growling against the gravel beneath us.

"Almost there." Hilary said with a tone that could have been fear or excitement, or a combination of both.

"Yeah, it's off the beaten path alright." Mike replied lightheartedly.

My eyes strained through the dark night to see something, anything, that might give a sign of the infirmary being close. Hilary pointed and I caught a glimpse of a pinpoint of light ahead. Focusing on it, the rest of the world slipped away as if I had died and were floating ever closer to the light that so many people who have had near death experiences speak of. As we drew near, I recognized it as a dusk to dawn light, surrounded by large trees. Still a hundred yards away, it called to us like the beacon of a lighthouse on a foggy bay.

The quiet and low hanging clouds let go of a cold and steely November rain as if it were expecting us, waiting to unwelcome us and send us away. Creeping ever closer, I could see the electric blue glow of the metal halide light perched high atop a creosote soaked wooden pole. The faint blue unveiled a small gravel parking lot and a split in the road.

I could see from my back seat perspective that as the road made a slight upward grade, an even narrower drive jutted off to our left just before the lighted trees and in between the road we traveled and the askew lane was a one lane entrance to the gravel lot. The truck slowed to a crawl and slowly made the half turn toward the lot entrance. Without warning, the bouncing headlight beams switched to bright and the towering infirmary peered out from the trees, angry at our late night arrival. The vacuum of darkness in its windows stared at us, taunted us, and seemed to curse our very presence.

The truck nosed into its parking spot near the light pole. This would give us not only ample lighting to begin to unpack some of our equipment, but also offer some security from any potential wandering vagrants or coyotes. We sat silently for a moment glaring out through the trees at the ominous structure that awaited us. A feeling of dread filled the cab of the truck and our spirits were dampened before we ever stepped foot out into the cold misty rain.

"Well... we're here." Hilary solemnly stated the obvious, if for no other reason than to break the silence.

"That we are." Theo agreed. I could hear the concern in his voice.

"I'm no psychic, but I get the feeling something doesn't want us here." I had always played the 'third-eye blind' card. It was safer and less frightening to believe that the things I felt or even saw were merely intuition or imagination. It also helped me to properly conduct my scientific investigations and research with little distraction.

"I don't think you have to be psychic at this place." Mike chimed in. "We definitely aren't welcome. Everyone who has been here says the same thing."

"True..." Hilary agreed. "I hope the spirits here are active tonight. I think sometimes they 'hide' when someone who isn't afraid comes, just so they won't come back."

"Every situation is different, but I doubt they will all be able to hide from me." Theo said with the slightest of a grin.

We sat in the warm confines of the running pick-up while the wind shield wipers slowly tapped out a rhythm, and I prayed the rain would end before we had to drag our electronic gadgetry out into the unshielded vastness of the night. The radio had gone quiet, as did our conversation when the stuttered drag of the wipers alerted us to the ending of the shower. It was time. It was as if some silent alarm had gone off when all four doors opened simultaneously and we all stepped out into the cold night air. I shuttered and zipped my coat up tight to my neck and pulled my sock hat down low over my ears. Gloved hands began to fill pockets with emf detectors, K-II meters, digital recorders, and cameras. I turned on my Mel-Meter and checked the temperature and saw that the emf reading was a flat zero. I powered it down and placed it back in my pocket.

With flashlights in hand, as the adrenaline surged through my veins, we approached the menacing building. Four stories tall, and somewhat U-shaped, the structure seemed to grow larger with each footstep. Mike held the brightest light while the rest of us made our way over the plastic, orange barricade fence that surrounded the property. He followed behind and quickly caught up to us. The tall, dead grasses were drenched in dampness and chilled our feet as we trudged purposefully toward the infirmary with Hilary and Mike taking the lead. The beam of his light shone back and forth searching the exterior brick walls of the building for an entrance.

"There it is." Mike mumbled to himself and fixed his light on three limestone steps and an old broken down door. The door hung on its hinges and swung ever so slightly in the cool wind like a lifeless cadaver at the end of the hangman's rope. Pulling the door open to one side, Mike redirected his light to the interior and filled the space with a cold glow. "After you... Be careful and watch your step. This place isn't as safe and strong as it appears."

"Thanks." My voice was monotone as I passed him in the doorway. Searching around the room we had entered, I saw an opening to the left and another straight ahead. Hilary walked straight ahead and into the next room. Theo and I followed close behind her. The ceiling was a corrugated metal supported by bar joists and had a poured concrete deck above it. I knew this because I had the startling realization that this was not a safe structure when we filed into the area and found the ceiling to be collapsed over nearly one quarter of the large space.

"Something definitely doesn't want visitors here anymore." Hilary said to us and in the light of my LED flashlight her eyes looked glazed and empty. "We aren't alone." The words were hollow and cold, much like the room where we stood. The temperature was noticeably colder than it was outside. I retrieved my mel-meter and checked the readings. No emfs were present, but the temperature was a full eleven degrees cooler than it had been outside.

"Not only are we not alone. We are being watched." Theo added to the unnerving feel of the bedraggled structure. "Over there..." I snapped a few photos as he pointed past a decrepit easy-chair to one of two accessible doorways.

"Really?" Mike shivered. "That's the way we were going to go, and really the best access to the main structure where the inmate rooms are..." His words were slow and drawn out.

"I don't mind going first." I spoke up. "I only see an empty old building, so to me it isn't intimidating at all. Not yet, anyway." I tried to make light of not having any psychic abilities and hoped it would help Hilary find the courage needed to pursue this investigation. They all followed as I walked cautiously through the door and into a long hallway that went to my left and right. Mike quickly turned his light to the right and spoke.

"Through there." It was all he said, but I knew to follow his lead and take the hallway to the right and through the open arched doorway at the end.

The opening led us into another hallway that ran perpendicular to the first and we stood in dizzying wonder at the labyrinth that this building had rapidly become. Mike and Hilary flittered their lights around, searching for the correct doorway. Theo and I stood still, soaking in the history and the putrid feelings that oozed from the walls around us, while Hilary and Mike peeked into nearly a half a dozen doors.

"Over here!" Hilary called out.

Single file, we passed through the doorway, like a portal to another world, a dark and evil world. Before us rose a winding and twisting stairwell that spiraled up into the open darkness above. A huge window filled a portion of one of the exterior walls with numerous panes of cracked or broken glass caked with what appeared to be eons of filth and spider webs. The floor and the steps were littered with old paint chips that had peeled from the walls and ceiling and scraps of papers that were water-stained and nearly illegible.

"What the hell? I just swept this out a few weeks ago." Hilary puzzled.

I began to ascend the steps slowly and looking back over my shoulder, I could see the others waiting hesitantly.

"Best to let you get to the first landing before anyone else starts up. One at a time, just to be safe." Mike said as he glanced from Hilary to Theo.

One by one, step by creaking step, we found our way to the second floor of the infirmary. The dimness of my flashlight broke through the dark as I entered the second floor hallway. Eerie shadows, from discarded and broken furniture and decor, danced across the cold and barren walls. Footsteps came behind me, echoing slowly in the emptiness. Theo appeared first, followed by Mike. Hilary stood motionless in the doorway.

"I'm just going to wait out here. I don't know if it's such a good idea for everyone to be in the same area at the same time, considering the cave-in we saw downstairs." She whispered to us.

"Good point Hil." Mike nodded in accord. "In fact, if you guys want to take my light, I'll just wait here too."

"I have a light, thanks." I said though mine was far less bright. Looking over to Theo, I raised my eyebrows.

"You guy's keep it, in case you need it. I have one too." He drew a small penlight out of his pocket and with a click turned it on.

The stairs had led us up into the south west corner. The corridor opened to our left into the west wing and straight ahead to the front section of the infirmary. I began to wander from room to room, casually looking in each one to see if anything grabbed my attention, while Theo walked earnestly down the hallway toward the front of the building and its main entrance. I pulled myself out of the third doorway I had discovered and found Theo frozen in his tracks. The light beam, like a saber, stabbed out across from where he stood and into the main entryway and stairwell. I stood my ground and waited for him to make the first sound or move, but the first sound did not come from Theo.

"Click-Tap, click-tap, click-tap" the sound repeated and faded. Reminiscent of a wooden heel and leather sole of an old boot or dress shoe ascending the metal steps, the sound clamored through the air. Though I consider myself a brave soul, I feared what ghastly being might exit the stairs and expose itself to us. I glared forward and heard Theo suck in his breath with a gasp. Seconds passed like hours until, with a sigh, Theo exhaled.

"Wow..." His whisper filled the empty corridor. "Okay. We may need to regroup."

"Why? What's going on?"...besides the phantom footsteps, I thought as I neared where Theo stood.

"I said we weren't alone. That was an understatement. We are gravely outnumbered by spirits, but there is something darker here too... something malicious... something evil." His words were sharp and hit us all hard. Though Hilary already had known this, she had only now been truly validated.

Our heartbeats quickened and our breaths were deep and swift when the four of us rejoined at the stairwell door. The thoughts, possibilities, and our imagined fears whirred through our heads. We had only just arrived and already it had seemingly been brought to our attention that this haunting was as legitimate as any we had experienced. The other possibility was that an uninvited and unwelcome person had taken refuge in the infirmary, perhaps a homeless man or a drug addict. The thought of another person being in the infirmary was not good, but also not likely.

Our ears strained through the silence of the night until it almost hurt and the annoying ringing began to overcome the possibility of actually hearing an external sound. No sound could be heard by any of us except for the beat of our hearts and eventually the dull ringing. Mike raised his eyes and pointed his index finger upwards. I nodded, understanding that if someone or something were going up the main stairwell, our best bet was to also move upwards. I crept up the steps carefully, but not without a sound. Pausing with each step, I listened for any movement, but heard nothing. When I had reached the third floor landing, I waved my light over the edge to signal the next adventurer to begin their climb. Hiding my light, I walked silently into the open corridors, identical to the layout of the second floor. I kept watch and listened until I was joined by Theo. We each stood guard. I faced north, down the west wing corridor and Theo faced east towards the main entry stairs until we had all arrived on the third floor. Through a series of hand motions it was decided that we would split up and two of us would go in each direction. Mike and Theo took the west wing and Hilary and I began slowly searching the main hallway rooms toward the front stairs. We continued on, searching room by desolate and unremarkable room.

The four of us joined up at the same stairwell after nearly an hour of paranormal detective work that had left us empty handed. One by one we crept up the open, spiraling staircase. Gathering at the top, we separated into our twosomes again and thought it would be best to take the same areas as we had on the previous floor.

***

Hilary and I had chosen to take turns. While one of us entered a room and investigated it, briefly searching for visitors, clues and any unexpected bits of information, the other waited in the hallway and kept an eye and ear out for any sign of our stair dweller. Bit by bit we whittled our way through the main corridor pausing for a bit at the staircase to do a quick evp session in hopes of finding the answer to who may have been treading on the steps or recording these phantom sounds.

After a brief wait and a few questions asked, Hilary and I passed beyond the stairwell and on to the other rooms in the corridor. The closer we found ourselves to the east wing, the colder it began to feel. Crackling debris filled the silent space around us as I entered the last room before turning the corner into the west wing. Following the beam of my light, I peered around the room... a broken bed-frame and weather rotted mattress, scattered pieces of clothing, and empty bookcase...nothing of particular interest to me. I stuck my flashlight into my coat pocket and rubbed my gloved hands together. Turning back, I reentered the corridor.

I raised my hands to my face and exhaled heavily to warm the bare skin of my face with the heat of my own breath. The cloudy steam billowed forth from my mouth, now thicker than before. Hilary turned slowly towards me and I could see her breath escaping her open mouth. Her eyes were empty and yet still projected fear. From one of my coat pockets, I extracted my mel-meter and checked the temperature.

"This can't be right. This says it's fifteen degrees in here. It was nearly fifty outside." I spoke to Hilary, but her response made me question if she had, or could, hear me.

"We are almost there. Just ahead. They are waiting." Her sentences were stuttered and cold, lacking emotion and rhythm.

"Who is waiting?" I asked loudly. Dozens of thoughts filled my mind. 'Who is waiting' was only one of them.

"What do you mean?" Hilary asked curiously.

"You said, 'They are waiting'. Who did you mean?" I posed the question a second time.

"I did? I, I guess I was just mumbling nonsense. I was kind of 'zoning out' in the cold. All I remember thinking was that is seems a hell of a lot colder than it did earlier." She said, confirming that she hadn't hear a word I had said.

"It is colder. My mel-meter says it's about thirty-five degrees colder than it was outside. I have heard of cold spots, but this is a bit extreme." I spoke as I stepped toward Hilary and the corner of the corridor.

Hilary watched as I walked past her, but didn't move, only following me with her eyes. Every step, every inch, towards the east wing was like trekking through the arctic. The temperature seemed to drop with each passing second. Frost quickly grew on my gadgets until my meter and flashlight both refused to work any longer, just as Hilary caught up to me and we rounded the corner. Twenty yards outside of the far end of the east wing was where the dusk to dawn light stood. Its cold light fought its way in through broken windows and slightly ajar doors. We stood still at the corner looking through the east corridor to where shattered bits of light stabbed at the blackened walls and stained hardwood floors, but we began to see more. Slight movement in the darkness caught our attention and I raised my useless gadgets and Hilary raised her camera, afraid to whisper. Shadow figures emerged and multiplied. The frigid cold and fear had us frozen in place. We could do nothing but watch and wonder.

Photos by Hilary Lee

Chapter 5
SOMETHING WICKED

A dozen or more transparent shadow beings filled the corridor. Mesmerized, we watched as a door, just over half way down, slowly moaned its way open, but instead of cold light escaping through its opening, an icy black vacuum exuded from it and into the hallway behind the shadow beings.

"Do you need help? We can help you." Hilary stammered. "Maddie, are you here?"

The black nothingness grew beyond the shadow spirits and blocked out our view of the corridor behind it, filling the space with a darkness that nothing could escape. Though I could not look away from the gathering of shadows, I could mentally feel the icy crystals of frost growing, covering not only the emf meter in my hand, but my gloves as well. The corridor itself began to appear covered in wintery ice. My feet felt frozen to the floor, and the blood turned cold in my veins, growing through my extremities. I wanted to look over to Hilary, but I could not even move my frozen eyes to one side.

Hilary had managed to muster up strength that I did not have. With an energizing whir and a 'k-snick, k-snick, k-snick' the hallway filled with sound and flashing light of Hilary's camera. My flashlight flickered back on slowly, as if it had to warm up to full brightness and the corridor was suddenly barren once again. The immediate change in temperature from what must have been below zero to above forty, felt like a very welcome heat wave. I turned to face Hilary and could see the frosty ice crystals, like snowflakes on her eyelashes, melting into a steamy vapor.

"What the hell just happened?" I posed the question. I had experienced random cold spots, and my team and I had our meetings with the fiery spirit of Ashley Sue, but this was a whole new paranormal experience, unlike anything we had even heard of.

"You tell me... I feel like a flippin' popsicle!" Her teeth chattered as she spoke.

Hilary's shaking hands raised her camera and pressed the review button. I could see the beaded moisture, like dew, glistening on her Cannon X-1 camera. I watched as she pulled up the last photo taken. It was nothing but a blur of dull, earth-tone colors through the moisture on the lens. The previous picture was more blurred around the edges, but the center was a kaleidoscope, filled with the same colors, but more defined. With the electronic 'ting' of the scroll button, the third picture (actually the first one taken) filled the screen.

"Doesn't look like I had much luck." Hilary said with disappointment. "This one is nothing but colors through the frost on the lens."

"The way I see it Hil, we were about to be human icicles, and your quick thinking may have saved us from who knows what! I think that's pretty lucky." I tried to be encouraging while I began to move my feet that were no longer frozen to the floor.

64

"Okay...true... but what does it mean? Why did these spirits decide to gang up on us in the east wing? I have been here a dozen times and this is the first time I've ever been ganged up on and nearly frozen to death. I mean, seriously... what's that all about?" Hilary's voice was troubled and confused.

"It's a mystery to me too. I think we need to keep exploring this level and see if there is anything here that we aren't supposed to find." I said as I handed Hilary the mel-meter and retrieved a small, top spiral bound, pocket notebook and pen from my interior jacket pocket. I jotted down notes in an orderly time-line of detailed and broken sentences and a quick sketch of the third floor with an 'x' marking where we stood and a circle around the area where we saw the shadows.

Our investigation of the area became intensified. We no longer felt that it was a good idea to separate and entered the first room in the corridor. Just to the right of where we stood was the open door. The room was a basic fifteen foot square, mostly empty. There were two windows with only a few unbroken panes in the wall opposite of the door. In front of the windows were hundreds of shards of broken glass, and in the corners to the right were a scattered disarray of papers and broken bits of history. I scoured through the scraps of paper searching for any clue while Hilary shot video footage and countless still photographs. I found nothing of any legibility or significance.

As we wandered from the first room to the next one across the hall, Hilary spoke. "I wonder if Mike and Theo have had anything happen. They have been awfully quiet down there."

"Yes, they have." I began to wonder if they were okay, considering what we had just been through. "Do you think one of these shadow people we saw was your 'friend' Maddie?"

"Hard to say for sure, but I doubt it. She seems like a very introverted soul. I expect when and if we find her, she will be alone and hiding." Hilary looked down the hall. "Poor woman. From what I have found, she lived a tortured life, misunderstood and abandoned."

The second room was much like the first in this wing, mostly devoid, but we searched it anyway and came up empty handed once again. The next doorway was where we believe the ominous blackness had emerged from. Without a spoken word, we approached the door with intimidation. Although it was not closed tight, nearly two inches ajar, the door was stuck firmly. The door was hinged on the right hand side and would have opened inward, if I could have moved it. I leaned against it with all of my weight, but it did not budge. I held my light up to the opening and peered in. There was a dresser and a bookshelf that still held a few moldy and grungy books in its spaces.

"Is this a 'patient' room, or an inmate apartment?" I asked.

"This wing was for patients. The west wing's upper two floors were for 'inmate apartments', the second floor was for more intensive care, and the first floor of the west wing was where the inmates who were considered dangerous, or a threat to themselves or anyone else were housed, it's also where the 'paupers room' was located." Hilary had done her homework and knew the infirmary better than anyone else alive.

"Okay, then who do you think could have been in this room?" I queried, not sure if there were an answer that was more than just a guess.

"This wing was more for elderly folks and those who were either bed ridden or confined to wheelchairs...stuff like that. Every floor of this wing had one room designated for a full time professional. A nurse, psychiatrist, or some medical professional would have had a room here that they would sometimes even sleep in if they needed to. It's hard to say which room it was, but this room could have been a patient or professional room." Hilary thought, racking her brain for more details she had learned and possibly forgotten.

"So, the pro room... would anyone else have used the room?" I was asking, but mostly thinking out loud.

"No one was supposed to have access to those rooms because

66

they would keep some medical supplies, confidential files and information in them, but back when this place thrived. I'm sure there were plenty of orderlies with less than desirable reputations." Hilary backed away from the door, glancing around the east wing as she spoke. "Something doesn't feel right."

"Maybe that means we are on to something, huh?" I grinned at her, but her expression was as blank as an empty chalkboard. Every thought and emotion, except for possibly fear, had been swiftly erased.

With my flashlight shining into the room and lightening the chest of drawers, I leaned against the door once more. My cheek pressed firm against the cold grain of the wooden door when my eye was met by another. A very pale and hollow eye, a terrifyingly angry brow, and a harrowing sliver of a male face startled me, only inches from my own. With a scream of "Holy Crap!" I jumped backwards, almost landing directly on Hilary. With a side step, she had managed to avoid being bowled over.

"What!? What's wrong?" She screeched excitedly, a mix of thrill and fear of the unknown. "Did you see something?"

"Yeah... I ... I think so..." My words were shaky and escaped between the exasperation of trying to catch my breath. "Someone, or something is in that room. We have to get in there."

"Maybe Mike can help." Hilary thought out loud.

"Yeah... maybe.." I said, but what I was thinking was that I wasn't able to budge the door, and I didn't think Mike would have any better luck.

"So, do we just wait here for them to show up, or abandon our watch and go get them?" I wasn't sure what to do. All I knew was that I wanted in that room, as soon as possible.

"MIKE!" Hilary called out, but said nothing else.

I was about to make myself 'comfortable' (if that was even

possible) by sitting on the floor and facing the curious door and the potentially occupied room, when we began to hear a faint sound.

"Footsteps?" I whispered the question and Hilary nodded in reply. She looked to the intersection of the corridors out of the corner of her eye. Her eyes widened and her head slowly turned towards the corner as she slowly raised her camera. I hid the light of my flashlight by pressing the lens against my jacket, but not turning it off. Avoiding the clicking sound of actually turning the light off and allowing it to be ready to reveal whatever came around the corner, I waited. The moments passed so slowly that it felt as if time had nearly crawled to a stop. Nearly silent footsteps that had been nearly indistinguishable now sounded like slow motion horse hooves trotting down a paved lane. It became evident that we were hearing multiple footsteps. The growing anticipation, perhaps, raised the hairs on my neck. The stepping sounds grew more audible and closer. It was as if I could feel Hilary's discomfort with the situation. In my head, I visualized the location of the sounds, and I knew something was about to confront us...once again.

The faintest of shadow movement appeared before us, not shadow entities like we so recently had seen, but a slight darkening on the floor at the corner intersection of the corridor. I sucked in my breath and Hilary began snapping numerous photos. The camera's repeated flash gave the area the sinister feel of an approaching villain from a silent movie. With great expectation of the horror we were about to face, we steadied ourselves as Mike and Theo rounded the corner.

"What the heck is going on here?" Theo asked, searching for the reason behind our unnerved behavior.

"We didn't know what was about to come around the corner, and well...we were preparing for the worst." I answered.

"Didn't you call me? I could have sworn I heard you call out 'Mike" or was that something else?" Mike began to question what else could have called out his name.

"It was me that called your name." Hilary said. "I didn't know if

68

you could hear me, but we didn't want to leave this spot."

"*Really?*" Theo asked. "Did you guys have an experience here?"

Hilary looked over to me and as frightening as our 'experiences' had been, we both grinned. We went into a long, drawn out and detailed account of what had happened. The tale passed back and forth between Hilary and I, and we tossed details into each other's accounts and even finished the other's sentences when we felt we needed to elaborate on certain aspects of the phenomenon. Though there were moments that I am sure the accuracy of our story was questioned, in the end, we were all on the same page as to what our next move needed to be.

I finished my tale with "...and so, that door must be opened."

Mike and Theo approached the door and pressed against it in turn, neither budging it in the slightest. Having the brightest light, Mike shone it through the crack, and as he did I cringed, recalling the ghastly face that I had been confronted with. No apparition appeared, which made me feel at ease, but also caused me to wonder if our story was losing credibility with Mike (being the most skeptical of our foursome).

"It's stuck tight." I stated the obvious.

"We need leverage." Mike thought for a moment. "I think I have an idea. Wait here, I'll be right back." And with that, he turned away and disappeared around the corner from where he and Theo had come.

"Soooo... I guess we wait." Theo said trying to lighten our mood. While we awaited his return, the three of us spoke about the incidents that had brought us to this room, and explored what mysterious revelations, if any, might be hidden within this room. Several minutes passed before we heard Mike's steps returning up the main stairwell and through the corridor. When he rounded the intersection, he carried a thick walled metal pipe, nearly two inches in diameter and seven or more feet in length.

"This will get us in there." He paused. "I think."

"It should." I agreed. My background in science had taught me that with proper placement and force, leverage could move mountains. "Let's get to it then."

Mike handed his light to Hilary, and I handed mine to Theo. The pipe was wedged into the open crevasse and while Mike pulled at the pipe from the left, hallway side, I pushed from the right, door-jamb side. It moaned, groaned and did not give even the slightest. We paused briefly and I thought. Raising a finger in the air, I alerted Mike to give me a second to reposition the pipe. Once in place, I instructed him to place his foot against the wall and pull with everything he had. I could hear and feel Mike straining with all of his might as I pushed from the opposite side. The force was greater, but still not enough.

"Keep pulling!" I instructed Mike. I backed off a few steps and with a burst of adrenaline, I lunged at the door, throwing myself against it. With a loud bang the door broke free and flung open fully. Mike fell backward with the old pipe and landed flat on his butt, squarely in the middle of the hall. The old infirmary let out an echoing shudder. Dust trickled down from the ceiling above and filled the air. Before us lay the secret room; a ghoulish prison of mystery and intrigue. I had half expected this 'face to face' fiend from my earlier encounter to come flying, floating, or rushing out to confront us in anger and fury. There was no apparitional appearance; no blood curdling scream. All was quite normal, and for Hilary and I, it was the furthest thing from our expectations.

Theo and I cautiously entered the room and began searching and investigating the defunct space. Though there were a few scattered papers, a chair, and a broken down old bed my attention was captivated by the chest of drawers that remained intact.

"I think the dresser may hold some importance, but I don't know if it is in the contents, or its energy." Theo remarked.

"I know what you mean. I saw it through the crack, and even if I hadn't had any paranormal experience here, I still would have had to get this door open, just to check it out." I agreed with him, but had to ask a question that was a conundrum to me. I have never considered myself psychic in any way, or even sensitive, but there are moments when something strikes me a certain way, brings out some specific emotion, and I constantly question if it is my brain tricking me by bringing up bits of old memories, or if I am actually feeling an energy or embedded emotion or tragedy associated with the 'thing' in question. Scientifically, I understand that the mixture of many elements such as smell, time of day/night, visual perception, texture, and many other elements combined with memories, whether they are personal or simple something from a movie or book, can give us all specific feelings about a place, object or experience, even if it seems to be something new to us.

"It's not the old broken bed or even the face that I saw in this room, but something about it just gives me a very bad vibe. Is it just me, or are you picking up on anything?" I felt awkward about even asking, but as a scientific researcher I knew that the best way to understand something is to ask as many questions as possible and formulate a theory.

"Well..." Theo started slowly. "I was going to say that I feel a lot of negative energy in this room, but I don't feel a presence here anymore. What I am feeling could be residual energy from the entity you saw here earlier." He paused and I scrunched my eyebrows at him, though I knew he could not see me in the dark that surrounded us. "I would have normally waited to say anything, but yes... how do I put this... I feel drawn to the chest and I don't feel real negative energy from it. It's more like I am being persuaded to explore it, rather than drawn to it by the energy of the chest. Now, that being said... there is a lot of anger, humiliation, and pain associated with this bed. The amount of 'bad vibes', as you called it, is overwhelming. It makes me very uncomfortable and not only do I not want to touch it, I don't even want to go near it."

"I understand pal. If you will hold the light on it, I'd like to take a closer look at it." Without another word, Theo poised the light so that its dim beam illuminated the nearest side of the bed. As I approached it, I began picking up the scattered papers on the floor and sorted them neatly, just another hint of my OCD coming to light in this dark and dismal place. With each paper I retrieved from the floor, I unfolded any edges and tried to choose the front side to put 'face up' as I began collecting.

The bed frame was iron tube, and not particularly interesting... definitely a standard type for this facility. The mattress was so old, stained and dry-rotted, that I doubt it held any real clues, but I couldn't help but notice the tears in the fabric went in several directions and radiated from near the center. I found this quite odd and interesting enough to take note of. Curiosity had the best of me and I pulled my flashlight from my pocket. Tuning it on, I laid it on the floor directed at the bed and with one hand on the floor and one under the mattress, raised the grungy and tattered piece up, pressing my cheek against the grit and filth of the hardwood floor, to inspect the underside. Much to my amazement, the bottom side was very much intact, though still aged and weather stained.

A scratching and scurrying sound appeared in such close proximity to my face, that I dropped the mattress and lunged backwards onto my butt. I felt the color leaving my face, though it quickly returned in an overabundance when Theo and I both saw a field mouse dart from under the bed and flee to its next 'not so safe' haven under the old chest of drawers. When I regained my dignity, Theo and I both had a bit of a chuckle.

"What's so funny?" Hilary's voice echoed from the corridor, and I was almost too embarrassed to admit I had been more frightened by a mouse than being eyeball to ghastly eyeball with a displaced soul.

"A very small 'entity' rushed at me from under the bed, and we just kinda thought it was funny." I didn't exactly lie. A mouse is an 'entity' by definition.

"I was terrified! It was a small four legged furry entity with a long hairless tail." Theo clarified the situation, which drew an "OH GAWD!" from Hilary and what I believe was intentionally excessive laughter from Mike.

"Well Theo, the chest is all we have left to explore, and the mouse

72

ran under it." I spoke through the intermittent laughter and snickers from Mike and Hilary. "Do you want me to hold the light on this one?"

"Naw, I've got it, you just make sure I can see in the drawers and show me whatever you find. I feel like there is going to be something significant in the bottom drawer." He motioned with the flashlight circling its beam around the face of the lowest drawer.

His particular interest to the bottom drawer filled me with anticipation, but it also caused me to extend that anticipation by beginning my search at the top drawer and working my way down. Though not 'well oiled' the upper drawer opened without much effort. Theo raised his light as did I. Getting down on one knee for a closer inspection, I found the drawer to be well crafted, solid wood, and, aside from cob-webs and dust bunnies, quite vacant. We noticeably and simultaneously exhaled upon the disappointing discovery. I moved on to the second drawer and found the same disappointment. Our hopes were failing when the third drawer was opened to reveal only an abandoned nest and scattered rodent droppings. All too quickly, I had reached the last drawer which we had been anticipating. Our expectations were far from high when I reached for the drawer handles.

Theo, who had been hunched over more and more as the search worked its way downward, suddenly stood up and turned his light quickly from side to side. Though I still had my flashlight on, and held it between my thighs as I reached for the handles, I wondered what could have possibly been important enough to distract him from our potential find.

"Hurry." He whispered the one word, and I had no doubt he meant it with good reason. "Hurry!" he said again in his full and demanding voice.

I tugged at the drawer, but it was stuck, only opening about a half of an inch. I attempted to wiggle it back and forth, up and down, even twisting it to every possible degree and angle, but at the most it opened just over an inch.

"Something isn't right." Hilary called from the hallway. "We need

73

to take a break and get ourselves out of here for a while."

"Just a minute...one more drawer." I called back over my shoulder.

Photos by Rick Kueber

CHAPTER 6
THE CLIFF HANGER

I gave one last firm tug and as I did more dust trickled down from the ceiling above and the infirmary itself gave a dying moan. Our mouse friend showed his true colors and fled to the corridor just as Theo and Mike screamed out in unison, "RUN!"

I scrambled out of the door just behind Theo. A groaning sound, like the bending and breaking of a large tree in a storm, filled the air, followed by ear stabbing pops and cracks. The dust flew and the ceiling gave way over head as we entered the hallway. Mike and Hilary had already escaped around the corner and were swiftly approaching the center stairwell. They paused long enough to silently question whether to trust this staircase or continue to the one at the end of the hall. As they did their hearts sank when the sound of an obvious cave in rumbled down the corridor followed by a billowing cloud of dust so thick even Mike's bright light could not penetrate it.

"Oh my god!" Hilary whimpered. "Oh god...I hope they are okay."

She said, but the words had only left her lips when she heard a sound she held mixed emotions about.

"HELP!" Theo shouted at the top of his lungs.

Mike and Hilary both had hoped that Theo and I would emerge from the cloud of dust, but that would not be the case. They stepped very lightly, as if walking out onto a pond of thin ice. The floor seemed solid enough, but the air was still foggy with the settling dust and restricted their clear view.

"Hil, please... just wait here. Let me go first." Mike said, putting on his brave face. He did not want to leave his wife behind any more than he wanted to venture forward into potential disaster, but cries of help tugged him onward.

"Okay, but remember, I'm going to be here all alone in the dark...please come back for me." He could hear the worry in her voice and in the flickering of his hand-held light he caught the sight of her eyes watering up, though he knew if he said anything, she would blame it on the cold and the dust.

"I..." He started to speak but couldn't find the words.

"Just hurry and come back to me safe." She said and he stopped his clumsy sentence.

He turned his light back down the hallway and with a few steps he disappeared around the corner. Just as he did, her ears caught the sound of the words he struggled to get out past his emotions.

"I love you Hil." and then he was gone.

***

Right on Theo's heels, I raced out of the room. It was much as many people describe a car accident or other major catastrophe... everything happened in slow motion and the calamity was muffled in my ears. The sound of my own deep breaths and the pounding of my adrenaline filled heart overtook all other auditory sensations. The floor gave way nearly beneath our feet and we were forced to turn the opposite way in the corridor. Small bits of concrete floated down as the ceiling above began to crack like lightning crossing the night sky. In spite of time seeming to have slowed, we watched and felt the raining debris, small at first, but quickly escalating to a terrifying disaster. A large slab of concrete and iron re-bar, several feet in diameter, came plummeting from above and crashed through the floor immediately behind us. The entirety of the Infirmary shook and trembled in the aftershocks of the imploding structure. I was terrified, and it seemed that death was inevitable. Inevitable or not, I was not ready or willing to make that transition.

My life flashed through my mind when I felt the floor give way beneath me. The better part of the ceiling, the exterior wall, and roof above, as well as the floors below were gone. Just past the room we had been in was a doorway and just before that doorway, the floor split and folded over limp, like a broken tree branch. Only the re-bar held it in place and kept it from falling to the ground level far below. I fell forward as the structure beneath me gave way. Falling hard on my chest, my arms stretched out in front of me. The slab of concrete floor began to tilt away from the door and the crack grew larger. I could feel gravity taking hold of me and trying to pull me down to the pile of rubble below. Scrambling, my fingers reached the crack...my left hand first and then my right. The shards of busted masonry dug into my fingers and hands as I attempted to pull myself away from the chasm of doom below. I fought through the pain of the cuts and tears on my hands as I gripped and pulled with all of my might. It was no use. I lacked the strength and energy to pull myself to safety. My only choice was to hold on for my life and hope that the others were okay and would come to my aid. Gritting my teeth and exhaling forcefully an unrecognizable vocalization, some cross between a cry and a grunt, and a spattering of saliva shot from my clenched mouth, not unlike a rabid dog.

It was just at this moment that two things happened, simultaneous and polar opposites. I looked over my shoulder at what lay beneath me to weigh my chances of survival if I could not hang on. The dim 'dusk to dawn' light that reflected off of the out building crept in, ever losing its power to enlighten by intrusive trees and branches, overgrown weeds and the orange barricade fence. What scarce light reached the debris below me revealed very little, but enough. I could see that the distance to the pile ranged from about twelve to nearly thirty feet below. I could also see splintered wooden beams and busted concrete slabs like taunting stalagmites below. I also knew there were hidden dangers like the iron re-bar that I could also be impaled on. I held on tight with my hands, but my hope was losing its grip. It was in this very moment that my mind drifted to the past and to my friend Tabitha. I had hidden (though not very well) a terrible crush that I had. When I was with her, or even texting with her, I felt like a kid in school, bumping shoulders with the girl of his dreams. She had a way of making me feel carefree and happy without even making an effort... and as obvious as it may have been, I had never told her. Right then, I had made myself a promise. If I made it out alive, I was going to tell her... something. I wasn't sure what I would say, but I wasn't going to hide my feelings any longer. Life was too uncertain for hesitation. In that same moment of mortal revelation and heart-sinking, inevitable doom, there was an uplifting sound.

"Rick? Are you there?" It was Theo, and though his voice was shaky, it came from above me, and that was promising.

"Here!" was all I could grunt out, but it was enough.

Theo laid down on the corridor floor and inched his way over to the edge until his head cleared the bounds of the missing floor where I hung. Looking up I could barely see his head and shoulders in the darkness, but I felt his smile telling me everything would be okay. His arms reached over and grabbed me around my wrists. Once he had a hold of me, he called out for help.

"I don't know how long I can hang on, but this is a lot tougher than it looks in the movies." I joked through my despair.

"Help!" Theo called out again as he switched his grip, clenching my left wrist and forearm with both hands.

"Hey!" I heard Mike's familiar voice change from elation to

concern. "Holy flippin' hell!" He said as his light bounced around the situation. I could only assume he was making a few short paces back and forth trying to decide what he could possibly do. "If you can hold on five minutes, I'll be right there."

Mike spun quickly around and bolted back down what was left of the corridor, now covered in dust and debris, and nearly trampled over Hilary as he flew around the corner.

"Oh jeez!" Mike exclaimed as he bumped straight into Hilary and came nose to nose with her for a fraction of a second. "Come on... Come with me. I need your help." He brushed past, taking her hand in his as he continued to rush down the corridor towards the furthest stairway. Without hesitation, Hilary took his hand firmly and trotted along through the dark hallway behind him, trying to watch the light beam for bits and obstacles that could catch her by surprise if she were to stumble over them unknowingly.

"Where are we going?" She quizzed him as they reached the stairway and slowed down for their own safety. "Are they okay?"

"They are okay for now. That's why we are in a hurry. Gotta go to the other side to help." Mike spoke in slightly broken thoughts and sentences.

"How are we going to help? Are they trapped? Did they fall?" Hilary's mind was running rampant through the possibilities and the severity of what had happened.

"Nobody fell, not yet." Mike said as they reached the ground floor and rushed out to the pauper's room area. "Take this light, go out to the truck, get the rope out of the back, and meet me on the fourth floor on the east wing...and please hurry."

With those words, in that dank, cold place, their eyes met. Mike kissed her quickly but not without passion, and hurried off into the shadowed distance. Before he disappeared, Hilary turned and ran out of the door to the surprisingly warmer air outside. Once out of the infirmary, the weight of everything lifted and she broke out into a near sprint tearing through the tangles of overgrown weeds and brush. Slamming against the barricade fence, she climbed, straddled, and then fell to the other side. Though she had twisted her ankle in the fall, she felt no pain. Past the fence, the dash to the truck for the rope and back were without hindrance. With her arm through the rope coil, and it slung over her shoulder, the passage back over the fence went much smoother.

Hilary's pace slowed when she reentered the cold, dark interior of the infirmary. There was an uncomfortable weight that came within the confining walls of this place. She could feel it over the urgency of the situation that compelled her. Her pace slowed once inside, but she walked with purpose and even ran when she entered the wide open space of the east wing corridor. The east stairwell was a bit of a different story. The handrails had been broken and cut off at their base and it struck terror into her before she was half way up the first flight. Hilary paused, pushing her backside against the wall, and found herself frozen. Every step she had taken only increased the dread that at some point she would fall over the unprotected edge of the stairs. Perhaps it was some deeply buried childhood trauma that paralyzed her with fear, or could it be that some supernatural force was making her feel this way... perhaps something wanted to push her over the edge; wanted her to not bring the rope; wanted none of us to be there, and now that we were, wanted none of us to leave...ever.

As these thoughts and frightening ideas scurried through her mind, she was suddenly gripped by a greater purpose and ideal. She was on a mission that was more important than her fears, and found the courage to overcome them one step at a time. With her back dragging against the peeling paint of the rough, plaster walls, something caught her jacket and threw off her balance. For only a fraction of a second, she thought she would fall to the floor far beneath her and it nearly drove her to tears. In that very moment, she knew I was hanging on for dear life at the other end of the stairs and corridor above. Hilary gathered her senses and stepped away from the wall, turning to face the rising stairs before her. Slowly at first, she began climbing. With every step, her pace quickened until she was moving so swiftly that she no longer even thought of falling, only of saving her friend.

80

Mike called out to her as she neared the top of the stairs. "Hurry Hil!"

Hilary burst through the doorway at the top and the shock of what she saw was unexpected. Just to her left, Mike and Theo lay side by side on the floor, hanging their arms over the edge of the rift in the infirmary. The hole was gaping and her sudden fear of falling returned without warning.

"I'm here Mike. I've got the rope...now what?" She said not being able to think clearly.

"Stretch out about fifteen foot of it. Double it over and then make a loop where it's doubled. And make a second loop near the end. Understand?" Mike shouted over his shoulder.

"Please hurry... we're all getting tired, and I need coffee." I grunted out, trying to make light of what was probably the worst situation I had ever been in.

"Got it." Hilary yelled back. "Now what?"

"Toss the looped end over the edge. I'll get it in place from there." Mike answered her and was almost instantly struck in the back by the rope as it flew past him and over the edge. It was right there, but I could not loosen my grasp and take hold of it...but I didn't want to die either.

"More!" Theo called out. "Need more rope." He had figured out Mike's plan as soon as the rope went over the edge. Hilary unwound more of the braided climber's rope and began feeding it over the edge. Inch by inch it was lowered until Mike called out.

"Okay, stop." He looked down and said calmly, something that sent me into a near panic. "Theo is going to let go of you and move the rope so that it is lying next to you, Rick." As cold as it was, Mike ungainly wiped the sweat from his forehead against his shoulder. "What you are going to do is put your foot into the loop at the bottom of the rope and let me know when it's in."

"Uh...okay, I'll try." I said. My voice was shaky and quiet. I held my breath as I felt Theo's white knuckle grip release from my arm, and then exhaled when the rope bumped against me. My feet struggled to get the rope into place without being able to see it. Having it between my feet, I fumbled about, trying to mentally picture the rope and loop. As I worked my feet around the knot and loop, somehow my foot accidentally slipped into place. Reflexively, I pushed down with my foot and felt the rope give freely. I stopped immediately in fear.

"Got it." I said, breathing deeply and feeling the tiniest bit of relief.

"Hil... you and Theo get on the other end of that rope and hold on with everything you've got." Mike instructed them before directing his instructions to me. "Okay, here's the plan... I'm gonna let go..." My heart sank as the words left his lips. "...you are going to hang on and when we pull the rope up about a foot, you stand up in the loop and then grab the rope."

The time ticked away slowly. These last few seconds felt like an eternity and for the first time since opening the door to the mysterious room, I felt that something was watching me...from below. I could hear the muffled talking of my friends above and felt the rope tighten and pull against the bottom of my foot, raising it until my knee bent.

"Okay Rick, we're ready." Mike called out.

I flexed my leg, straining against my exhaustion. My muscles were trembling but I managed to push myself upwards and as terrified as I was, I managed to pry my grip from the busted concrete slab, and snatched at the rope. My hand grasped the upper loop of the climbing rope. It had been perfectly placed and I don't believe I was ever more grateful. As sure as I was of my friends and the plan, I could not let go with my second hand. It was like my safety back-up, at least it gave me some mental security.

"Now what?" I asked as loudly as I could muster.

"Hold on tight, we're gonna pull you up." Mike's voice was far more confident than I was. "Ready?" He asked everyone rhetorically.

"Now!" And with that, everyone grunted and groaned, including me. The gritty dust ground between me and the broken floor as I was being pulled up. Though it was only a couple of feet, it felt like being air-lifted from the floor of the Grand Canyon. I held on tight until I was fully on the floor above, and even then I asked for "More..." until I had been dragged a few feet from the edge. I rolled over on my back and breathed a sigh of relief.

"You can probably let go of the rope now." Theo said sarcastically.

"Yeah, not just yet..." I said slowly. "If this is what that spirit-guide-eagle-thing meant by looking from a higher point of view, being courageous and being prepared to fly, I think I want a different spirit guide."

"Was it my imagination, or did someone mention coffee a few minutes ago?" Hilary joked.

"I did say something about coffee, but that was when I was hanging on for dear life, like six hours ago." I kidded back. "Is there a Starbucks in the other wing of the infirmary?"

"Unfortunately not, but there is one about fifteen minutes up the road." Mike smiled.

"Starbucks... fifteen minutes away... oh my god, that sounds so good right now." I day dreamed about a hot vanilla latte as I lay there still staring at the ceiling. "I don't suppose they deliver..."

My statement raised a few laughs, which was a comforting change from the seriousness of the situation we had all just experienced. Eventually I made myself crawl a few more feet from the edge and when I was comfortable enough, I stood up and my wobbly legs took me to my friends. In hind sight it seems corny, but a group hug was in order. My legs strengthened and my nerves calmed as we carefully made our way down the east staircase, which mirrored the one we had ascended in the west wing. I'm sure my friends got tired of hearing it, but I must have said 'thank you' a hundred times on the way to the truck and on the way to Starbucks.

Minutes later we found ourselves gathered around a table waiting for our names to be called out, announcing that our orders were ready. Others were called out by name but I hardly noticed until "Rick...Vente French vanilla Latte" snapped me back to reality. We sat mostly in silence and our eyes rarely met as we sipped at our hot refreshments.

"So...now what are we going to do?" Theo finally broke the silence.

"Well, I guess I'll have to make the call and tell them there was a cave in. He's not going to be happy." Hilary was speaking about the owner of the infirmary property.

"This is definitely going to throw a wrench into the restoration plans." Mike added.

"I keep getting the feeling that this has 'ruined' the night for you guys. I'm sorry that you drove all day to get here, and only had a couple of hours of investigating... that sucks." The disappointment showed on Hilary's face and in her words.

"Oh..." I was surprised. "I thought we were going back after we finished our coffee." I spoke in a generalization, as none of us were drinking 'just coffee'... vanilla latte as always for me. I also believe that I shocked everyone, as all eyebrows raised when I mentioned returning, and I think Theo almost spit out his drink.

"Seriously?" Theo said when he finally finished choking. "Are you sure you want to risk going back... I mean, it's obviously a very volatile situation."

"No kidding." Mike added. "We can go back if you want, but we are going to have to be extra careful anywhere we go inside. If it happened once, it could happen again."

"Yes, it could...but how are we going to get to the bottom of this haunting and help all of these poor souls?" The words came from my heart and helping souls, living and passed, was our purpose as paranormal investigators.

"You're right." Theo's words were slow and his tone was quiet. "I certainly feel like they aren't there by choice. Maybe they were once, but not anymore."

The conversation took a moment of silence as we all contemplated the dangers and the rewards that we were anticipating. Without saying anything, we looked back and forth at each other, each of us waiting for another to break the silence. It seemed like no one would follow Theo's statement, knowing it was most likely very accurate.

"Coffee to go?" Hilary said as she stood up unexpectedly.

"Yeah... good call." I agreed, I needed more caffeine to jolt me back to reality and back into investigation mode. "I think I'll just have regular coffee this time."

"I don't know if that's possible here, but I'll see what I can do. How about four 'regular' coffees? Is that alright with everybody?" Mike said as he joined Hilary, standing up. We all agreed and took our steaming, 'to go' coffees to the truck and sipped slowly at them as we drove the short distance back to the infirmary.

Photos by Rick Kueber

CHAPTER 7
TREAD LIGHTLY

Before any of us were truly ready, the truck was pulling into the gravel parking lot and the ominous infirmary loomed over us. A moment of doubt and paranoia filled me and knotted my stomach. Something inside of me was saying that this place, these spirits, this blackness we had seen, were all laughing at me, taunting me and daring me to enter their domain. For a moment, I thought these entities could kill any one of us if they wanted too, but then it occurred to me... if that was true, they could have easily done that when I was hanging white knuckled about to fall. One more bit of falling concrete could have sent me to my demise amongst the destruction below. My courage and my desire began to return.

I was actually the first to open my door and abandon the safety of the warm truck. Safety...ha...an illusion, I know, but it certainly felt safer with the heater blowing and the radio playing low. The cold wind now cut through me like stabbing needles, stinging my ears and face with the sudden reappearance of fine drizzling rain. I tested the hand-held gadgetry to assure myself that I wouldn't find one of them powerless, with dead batteries, once deep inside this dismal fortress of despair. The others soon joined me, and we began our short trek through the tangles of overgrown brush to the uninviting infirmary entrance.

"Are you sure you want to do this?" Mike posed the question to everyone one last time before reentering, reminding us of the apparent risks we would be taking.

"This place is dangerous, creepy, flooded with spirits and paranormal activity... of course I'm sure I want to go... not that I like it, but I'm sure we need to do some more digging and find any answers we can." Theo had a comical, yet no nonsensical point of view, and he was right. We could not discard the tormented souls who were here. They needed help, and that was why we were here.

"Agreed." I put my two cents in. "We may not figure everything out, or even 'fix' anything tonight, but I think we have more to learn before we leave."

"I'm okay with going back in, but I have two requests: One, we separate into groups of two again. I don't think it's a good idea to all be in the same place at the same time. We need to be aware of everything, watch where we step, and keep an eye out for any signs of another collapse." Hilary was obviously nervous about more than just the soundness of the structure.

"And what was the second thing?" Theo queried.

"Sage... I am going to light a sage stick and keep it with me at all times. I have two, and I think it would be best if both 'teams' kept one burning." Hilary added. We were all familiar with sage burning and smudging, and the properties that burning sage had. It had been used for centuries to ward off evil spirits and clear an area of negative energies. It was a tool that many used, some believed in, and we were putting our faith in.

We slowly passed the three steps to the entry and found ourselves back inside the icy grip of the infirmary. As we entered, Theo mumbled a prayer of protection to the saints asking them to watch over us. I wasn't sure if this made me feel better or more concerned, knowing that out of all of us, Theo saw and knew more of what we needed protection against. Our footsteps seemed alarmingly loud as we trampled through the collection of debris that littered the floor. Each of us had a scenario of where we were going, and who we would be going with, as well as what adventures, discoveries and horrors we might encounter. It was only when we reached the base of the first stairwell that we paused to make some sort of plan.

"Theo, do you want to go up to the fourth floor with me?" I asked.

"That sounds fine to me, if you don't think we want to split up and each of us go with someone who knows the layout of the place." He made a good point.

"Mike and I can go through the office areas down here and see if there are any useful documents that may have been left behind." Hilary offered.

"Okay... That sounds like a good idea...and if Rick and I are not accompanied by one of you, we won't have any information and direction, which could actually be a good thing." Theo pointed out again. "It could allow us to search someplace other that the 'usual' places you already have had experiences in."

"True." Hilary concurred. "Then take this with you and we'll meet you both back here in an hour, okay?"

"Sounds like a plan." I nodded as I took the sage stick from her and checked to make sure I had a lighter in my pocket.

Hilary and Mike headed slowly down the main corridor away from us and Theo and I entered the west wing stairwell and began our climb. I found myself still a little shaky as we rose higher in the unrailed staircase. Our assent was slow, but we kept a steady pace, stopping only briefly at each landing. During our pause at the second floor, while we looked and listened for any activity, I handed the sage and lighter to Theo,

89

which he immediately lit and blew out a few times in a row, until a billowing pillar of sweet, white sage smoke drifted upwards and filled the air with its pungent and calming aroma. Turning my light to shine down each corridor, on each landing, I found it slightly unnerving to see the new layer of settled dust from the recent collapse.

Eventually we reached the uppermost landing and the end of the rising black-iron steps. Peering left down the west wing corridor, a straight ladder that went through an opening in the ceiling caught my eye. The adventurer in me was returning. I longed to climb to the top and see what treasures were hidden in the attic of the aged infirmary. I caught Theo's stare and turned my light in the direction he was looking. Ahead of us was the main corridor, but he was looking slightly to his right. The beam of dim LED lights cut through the misty air and landed on a door that was somewhat ajar.

"She's there." The only words that left Theo's lips, chilled me to the bone. His eyes didn't blink, or waiver from their fixation on the door and the room that lay behind it.

"Who's there?" I couldn't help but wonder, and ask.

"The woman who needs our help... the one whose emotions are crying out the loudest...Madison..." Theo reached his empty hand out towards the door. "That was her room, where she lived, and where she...died."

The words painted a bleak picture of the spirit of Madison, but that was our whole reason for being here; to help her, and any others we may encounter. Theo waved his open hand over the sage stick several times and blew on it to rekindle the fiery cinders and cause the smoke to surge once more. Placing my light between my knees, I tapped him on the shoulder and held a finger up, gesturing him to wait while I retrieved my digital recorder from my inside jacket pocket and prep it for an evp recording session. I followed him to the door and watched as he effortlessly pushed it open with his one free hand.

The room was much the same as others we had seen. Bits of

90

trash and scraps of paper covered the floor, an old broken down bed was pushed up against the wall just to the right of a large multi-paned window, and an old built-in book case took up most of the wall to the left of the door. Even I could feel the sadness as I stepped into the room. It felt much like stepping off of a hospital elevator into the terminal ward; oppressive and hopeless. I laid my recorder on one of the empty bookshelves and stood silently as an observer, noticing that Theo seemed to be somewhere between worlds, still physically in front of me, but mentally and spiritually, he was somewhere else...somewhere distant.

***

"Madison..." He spoke softly. "Don't be afraid. We are your friends, and we are here to help you. What can you tell us?" Everything was different from Theo's point of view. At times he saw things differently than anyone else... he also saw things that I simply could not see, or even imagine seeing.

The thin frame of the young woman was sitting on the floor at the far end of the uncomfortable looking bed. Her knees were drawn up to her chest, with her arms wrapped tightly around them. Madison's face was buried in the small space between her knees and her chest, and her long, straight, and unkempt hair fell down over her spindly legs. Her head raised ever so slowly, and only slightly, followed by her eyes. Her gaze was fixed on Theo. Though she stared directly at him, it was as if she didn't believe what she was seeing. Her arms let loose and stretched out to either side, her hands, limp at the wrists. Though her lips never moved, her eyes spoke and Theo heard her voice within his own mind. The frail female voice in his head uttered a solitary word. "See."

Two rather large men in white button down shirts and white pants with shiny black leather shoes and belts materialized on either side of her holding her by the wrists. A scene was playing out before Theo, some emotional recording or residual haunting incident from her past. The men did not notice or see him, but he felt as if he was in the room on the day this moment occurred. The scuffling sounds, grunts and groans and voices were as clear as the day they were uttered. The smells of fresh shoe polish and of disinfectant and soiled linens infiltrated his senses.

"Come on princess... time to get you stripped down, scrubbed up and down in the therapy baths, then off to bed for you." One of the men said in a cruel tone.

"Princess? She ain't no princess, my friend. This here's Queen Madison, but I think 'Maddie' is more appropriate." Spouted the second orderly, his heartless sarcasm pained Theo, who could feel the hurt from within the young girl.

"Oh my! Well, beggin' your pardon madam. I didn't realize you were royalty!" The first man said as he let go a boisterous laugh.

"Yes... forgive him, your Royal Maddness!" The other taunted as they pulled her from the floor, unwillingly, and nearly drug her past Theo, dissolving into a cloudy mist as they passed through where I stood.

It was at that moment, when the newness of the infirmary, the two orderlies, and Madison began to dissipate, that the dark, dreary and fowl funk of the present reappeared. Our two realities overlapped for only a brief moment and I shivered as their shadows passed me by. For Theo, it was a snap back to the present reality.

"Not sure how this all adds into things, but I just saw two men, two infirmary workers, teasing Madison. They were calling her 'Maddie' and "Maddness' and they drug her out, against her will, to be bathed and to some kind of therapy." Theo explained his vision, giving only the basic details.

"I wonder what kind of therapy they were taking her to? Maybe for some kind of electroshock therapy?" I pried for more information.

"I really don't know, but it feels like it was a therapeutic bath or something like that. I wish she had given me more of a glimpse." Frustration was apparent in his voice..

Never making eye contact, Theo brushed past me and re-entered the corridor. I was unable to remain in the room. Something urged me to follow him into the hallway. Remaining a few steps behind, I watched cautiously as Theo meandered down the corridor a dozen or so steps before I called out for him to "Stop!". My flashlight remained poised just in front of his steps, watching for any dangers that he might not notice. I feared that Theo might be in some trance like state, or wandering in a vision that may not reveal the dangers of this reality. Theo halted and slowly turned back to face me, his hand pointing farther down the way.

"Down there...on the left... I think they took her in there." His voice was shallow but clear.

"If you'll wait here, I'll go take a look." I shook my light back and forth, flashing it across the floor in front of Theo. "You might want to back up a few steps. Doesn't look too safe."

Theo turned back to discover my light illuminating several areas of rot and decay, like the talons of some dragon or demon had torn straight through the floor in long slashing tears, amidst a scattering of debris, that showed through to the third story hallway below us. Nervously, I moved past him, stepping ever so slowly, feeling the firmness under foot before allowing the entirety of my weight to shift. The floor of this wing was wooden, and though not as heavily constructed as the other wing, it appeared far more decayed than the one that had collapsed beneath us. The quietest of moans was let loose as each step pressed heavily onto the spongy surface of the wooden floor. I held my breath between strides and only exhaled once I was assured I would not be plummeting through the floor.

There were two doors ahead, to my left, but I instinctively knew I was to enter the second door. The closer I was to the door, the heavier the air around me became, and the deeper the sadness in my heart grew...though I did not understand why. I stayed close to the left hand wall whenever the sturdiness of the floor would allow, scooting my feet across the floor, and feeling the grit of sandy dust scratching beneath me. When I arrived at the doorway, my back was pressed against the wall and my left hand and arm reached out pressing my fingers and palm against the slightly ajar door. I was surprised that it swung open nearly two feet with very little effort. I peered inside, scanning the floor and the layout of the room with my somewhat dim flashlight. The batteries were already beginning to fail in the frigid cold of the infirmary.

I slid farther against the wall, until I felt the door frame bump between my shoulder blades. I tested the floor just inside of the doorway with the toe of my shoe and soon found it to be quite solid. Shifting my weight, I stepped into the room and shone my now dim flashlight around to discern exactly what kind of room I had entered. The room was no larger than ten foot from the door to the window on the opposite side of the room and fifteen foot, or so, in the opposite direction. To my left were two standalone sinks and the wall just on the other side from the hallway wall was lined with partitions. It was a restroom, and obviously updated since the original days of the Infirmary.

I tapped the end of my flashlight and the beam momentarily grew brighter, casting its light across the edge of the partitions and creating eerie shadows and reflections against the far wall. Without warning, a shadowy figure, head and shoulders peeked out from behind the furthest partition and suddenly disappeared. I rushed to the end of the room, without thinking of the imminent dangers, to catch another glance of this otherworldly being, only to find it had disappeared without a trace. I retrieved the K-II meter from my jacket pocket and turned it on. There were a few weak flickers of light showing a minimal amount of trace energy that quickly faded, much like my light. I decided to make my way back to where Theo was before the batteries in my flashlight completely died.

On my return through the corridor of doom, I paused, noticing something that had caught my curiosity before. There as obvious as could be was the old wooden straight ladder that led up to an upper level, an attic and the belfry.

"You going up there?" Theo whispered loudly, nearly chuckling as he pointed to the small rectangular opening in the ceiling where the ladder disappeared into the nothingness beyond.

"What do you think?" I said with a smirk. "But, I'm going to need a better light. This one's about dead."

"Seriously?" Theo acted completely surprised by my response. "Do you think that ladder will hold you? It looks as sketchy as the floor" He nodded towards the dilapidated structure that I had been so cautious about only moments before... the same structure that the ladder was resting on.

Theo carefully walked up to the opposite side of the ladder and we exchanged lights through its rungs. It was then that I noticed the poor, degraded condition of the ladder. There was a better chance that it was completely dry-rotted than any chance of it actually supporting nearly two hundred pounds of weight. Regardless, I placed a foot on the bottom rung, and slowly tested it. It held. One panicky step at a time, I climbed, higher and higher. When I had nearly reached the top, I looked down.

"I'm either really stupid, or really brave..." I said to Theo who watched from below. "...but, honestly, I don't feel very brave right now." Though I couldn't see his face, I was sure he was grinning in agreement.

Turning back to the task at hand, I took another step. My head raised above the ceiling just as the rung underfoot made a loud pop. I was sure, once again, that I was about to die, but the rung did not break. It had only cracked, but it was enough to cause my legs to turn to rubber. I took one more step quickly and sat the light on the attic floor. Placing one hand on either side of the opening, I pressed hard against the floor, lifting my weight off of the ladder and rocked back, landing my butt onto the attic floor behind me. The floor looked quite solid. There was an area around the attic entry that was covered in wooden flooring. Ten feet beyond the ladder the rafters were exposed and fifteen foot ahead I could see where the loft turned to the left, which would have been above the front of the building. Several feet behind me was a red brick wall. It, and the underside of the roof structure were covered in a hundred years of spider webs and dust.

In the middle of the brick wall, and the middle of the wood covered floor, was an open arched doorway, and beyond that was a dark

95

unknown. I can't say if it was actually the temperature, but there was an unnerving coldness that poured out from the bricked opening. I was uncontrollably drawn to the bricked doorway. It was only about four and a half foot tall at the peak of the arch, and I had to duck to peer inside. My light only murkily lit the large space beyond. Instantly I felt I was in the right place at the right time. I was not alone in this attic, the far left corner exuded a frightening presence, but my eyes were pulled to the far right corner. My light brightened that corner only slightly more than the other, but as I scanned the rafters and upright supporting lumber, I gasped. What appeared to be the same shadowy figure peeked out from the blackish-brown uprights and though it had no eyes to be seen, it saw me. I could feel its stare piercing deep into my soul. I had something it desired, something it was confounded by, and yet distantly remembered... I had life. As I fumbled through my pockets to find my camera, there was a low moaning shriek, like the howling of an autumn wind through barren trees. As quickly as I could, I began to snap photos, hoping to capture an image of the ghostly figure, but it had disappeared as swiftly as before.

From the other corner, I felt the heavy coldness increasing, reaching out from its hiding spot. I turned my camera and snapped two pictures, but even the flash would not penetrate the evil darkness that flourished there. My camera immediately went dead and my light began to slowly fade. Some devilish creature took life from the shadows, the blackness spread across the walls like the spreading wings of a dragon. A monstrous figure formed from shadow, called me out by name, and its eyes were illuminated with a pale bluish glow. Fear was an emotion I was unfortunately familiar with, and this time it had gripped me so deeply, if I could have wished myself home and into my warm bed, I would have. I wanted nothing more than to not be there at that moment, caught in the gaze of this nightmare.

My light went out, and the beast called out my name once again. Though I felt nothing, I heard the flashlight hit the floor as I turned and ran the few short steps to the ladder and descended it so quickly I didn't have a moment to think of the frailty until nearly half way down when one of the rungs under my left foot broke from my clumsy weight. I paused only a fraction of a second before continuing on and reaching the remains of the floor beneath me. I did not stop, or even pause to check my footing, until I had passed Theo and reached the stairwell, where I met with Mike and Hilary who had just come up to check on us.

"Hey!" Mike called out cheerily.

"Everything okay? It's been more than an hour and we thought we should come check on you guys." Hilary added, feeling that something had me noticeably shaken and disturbed.

"I was wondering the same thing..." Theo said as he entered the stairs behind me. "What's the rush to get out of the attic?" Though he surely had some idea of my encounter.

"There was something up there... I saw this shadow, down the hall in that room you were talking about Theo, then I saw it again up in the attic..." I recalled the terror that had taken control of me, and the beast that had caused it. "There was something else though... I think it may have been the same thing we encountered in the other hallway, you know... before we went in the room, before the collapse..."

"Aw hell no!" Hillary expressed all of our feelings with perfect bluntness.

"We'd better go before the whole damn place falls in!" Mike motioned with his light toward the stairs.

Without question, or hesitation, we all descended the stairs and exited the Infirmary, never saying a word until we had reached the truck. Even then, we said very little as we loaded up and piled into the truck as it warmed up. Mike quickly backed the truck out of its parking spot, skidding to a stop and the tires spun slightly in the loose gravel of the parking lot when he switched to drive and sped forward out of the lot. We bounced onto the road and had a few miles behind us before Mike eased up on the accelerator and we finally began to talk.

"So, what the hell happened back there, and did you get any pictures?" Hilary asked.

"I took some, but I don't know how they turned out yet." I thought a moment and disappointingly said, "Well crap! I totally left my recorder in Maddie's room."

"I don't know if it's going to be a help, or if we'll catch anything, but I grabbed your recorder and had it going almost the whole time." Theo chimed in.

"Nice... It's got to be some help." I replied.

"Anyways..." Hilary sounded sarcastically annoyed. "What-the-hell-happened?"

I went about telling the tale of the shadow person appearing to me, watching me in both areas. They all listened intently as I spoke in great detail of the feeling I had during the encounters and how I felt compelled by the shadow, as if it needed help, but were afraid to make contact. When my story turned to the black winged beast, I thought that if it weren't for his seat belt, Theo would fall from his seat. There was definitely an evil presence at the infirmary. Whether there was any correlation between it and the murderous inmate who was diagnosed with a demonic possession as the reason for his sudden killing spree or not, I couldn't be sure, but what I did know was that this THING was almost definitely the same shadowy entity that we had encountered in the opposite corridor; the one who seemed to be in control of so many of the spirits trapped in that forsaken place. We spoke the entire way back to Mike and Hilary's home about the encounters, the collapse of the building, and the freezing cold. My thoughts and my input always circled back to the short chest of drawers and the bottom drawer that refused to open. I was certain there was some reason I was drawn to it, and I wouldn't be satisfied until I was able to open it, even if it was empty and contained no clues or answers.

My thoughts also returned to the moments when my life literally hung in the balance and the only person I could think of was Tabitha. During our conversations, I sent a social media text message to her. It simply said-

'Want to go for coffee sometime this week?'

She had always been a night owl and a second shifter, so I wasn't surprised to get a response before we made it back to their house.

'Penny Lane? :) Sounds good. Probably have to be next weekend... I work all week.'

Penny Lane Coffee Shop was where we had met the first time and I couldn't control my smile. I answered her back quickly before putting my phone back in my pocket.

'Awesome! I'll talk to you this week and we'll figure it out."

Photo by Hilary Lee

Photos by Rick Kueber

CHAPTER 8
DREAM A LITTLE DREAM

Theo and I were invited to stay at Mike and Hilary's for a bit of sleep before our long trek home, which is exactly what we did. It was nearly 4 am when we arrived, and though our minds buzzed, we all were exhausted and fell into deep sleeps quickly...

Rick

The couch proved to be very comfortable, and while I thought about the mysterious and terrifying experiences at the Infirmary, I dozed off into an eerie dreamland, where I feel I had been invited. This dream seemed to have a purpose. It was not just a dream; I was being shown a vision, and I knew exactly who was showing me these things.

I was standing on a grassy hill, sparsely dotted with maple and pin oak trees. The sky was a beautiful blue and the leaves of the trees rustled quietly in the spring breeze. I turned slowly to gaze down the hill to see the Infirmary and poor house below in the height of their existence. Common folks, paupers, and transients bustled about, tending to their chores, working the farm, and over all being content with their meager

101

lives... simply grateful to have a dry place to sleep and food enough to avoid starvation. An occasional man or woman in white uniforms would appear near the infirmary, some escorting a patient or inmate. Over all, considering the oppressive circumstances, it appeared to be a decent place full of kind people.

As I watched the daily lives of folks over a hundred years ago, a small hand reached up and grasped mine, taking me by surprise. I lowered my eyes to see who had joined me on this beautiful antebellum day. A sudden sickness hit the pit of my stomach when I recognized the child beside me, the child holding my hand, to be young Ashley Sue Helmach... the burning girl. My first thought was *'Why the hell is she here?'*, but I spoke not a word. Her piercing blue eyes stared deep into mine with a solemn sadness and without saying anything, and no cues, we both turned our gaze back to the Infirmary.

The Sky had grown dark and everyone had vanished. A light misting rain had begun to fall and the warm summer day had somehow changed to a dreary and cold, late autumn evening. A woman appeared from a distance struggling to carry a load that was almost more than she could bear. Without warning, I found myself, and Ashley, now standing near the front entrance to the Infirmary. The young woman, no more than twenty years of age, approached. Her faded blue cotton dress was ragged, torn, soiled and stained. Desperation and sorrow poured out from the woman like the putrid smell of death and rot one might experience far before finding a long dead animal on the side of the road. Raven black hair covered her face and was damp and matted. Raspy sobs of an unimaginable pain billowed from behind her mess of hair. We watched as she made her way slowly up the stairs, across the short, white bridge and to the massive, main entrance doors.

Unloading the mass from over her shoulder, I shuddered with remorse, seeing it was the body of a young boy. He lay there in the rain which was growing more steady. The desperate young woman beat her fists against the wood of the doors, trying to gain entry. She leaned over the boy and spoke to him with a voice hoarse from crying and sickness.

"Don't leave me Jacob... Please child. It's mum... stay with me a bit longer." She spoke as loud as her sore throat would allow as she began to beat on the door once again.

Relentlessly she pounded against the doors, and cried for help, each word shredding her throat more and more. The hours flew by, and with the passing of time, the night grew deathly cold. In spite of the cold, and her own sickness, the young mother pummeled her fists against the doors without relief, until Ashley and I could begin to see red marks of blood on the white painted front doors. A man peered through the window to the right of the door several times, but never unlocked or opened the door. My heart broke wishing I could just walk up and open the door for her, but I knew I was not part of this scene, only an observer of an occurrence long past.

I glanced to Ash, hoping somehow she could help, but when her saddened eyes met mine, I knew this situation would not be improving. Eventually the woman collapsed from exhaustion and we watched as the dawn began to break. Just before the sun rose, the front door opened and two men rushed out and dragged the young woman inside, leaving the boy behind. A short time later, the door opened again and another man exited, covering the child in a sheet and throwing him over his shoulder, he proceeded to walk around the eastern corner of the building to the caretaker's shed where he laid the boy in a wooden wheel barrow and placed a shovel in as well. Grasping the handles, the disheveled old man pushed the wheel barrow across the muddy road to a clearing near the woods and began stepping off paces, measuring a distance from the edge of the road and the woods. He stuck a stake in the wet ground and then grabbed up his shovel and began digging.

The grass and soggy ground turned easily beneath the weight of the untidy man and he soon had a hole two foot wide by four foot long dug. It was barely knee deep when he stopped and threw the shovel to the side. With cold hearted and careless apathy he snatched up the child and tossed him into the shallow grave. Once in the wormy hole, the man withdrew the sheet and placed it to the side while he shoveled the mucky dirt back into the hole saving the grassy bits for last, making sure to put them on top, grass side up so as to make the grave blend in more quickly. No marker was placed, no funerary rights were given. There was only the metallic scraping sounds of the shovel as it penetrated the loose soil and the grunts and groans of the weathered old caretaker as he added another shallow grave that would soon be forgotten by all except for a mourning mother who was not given the chance to say farewell to her only son.

The rain was drenching, cold and cruel, while I watched the travesty unfold. I felt as if my heart would break and the coldness would never leave me, when a sudden warmth filled my hand. Looking down, Ashley smiled up at me with watery eyes. The warmth of her grasp was comforting at first, but quickly the comforting warm became unbearable and I watched as the young girl burst into flames along with everything that surrounded us. I awoke with a start, covered in sweat, and noticed the sun was already up, though no one else seemed to be.

Theo

Theo, being a medium, had seen more than the rest of us during the investigation, and had experienced what we had, but more clearly. Despite all of the information to process, like us, he was utterly exhausted and soon fell into a near comatose sleep. Less than an hour into his slumber, his mind was awakened in a dream.

Theo found himself in a place most of us would not comprehend. It was not a physical place, but a place of emotion and energy. Swirling mists of every shade and hue imaginable filled this 'place'. Each unique mist represented its own emotion, feeling, and the energy type that was associated with it. He was aware as some brightest mists of the same type began to combine, representing love and happiness as fantastic events of joy took place; marriage, births, and the like.

This caused Theo's spirit to be uplifted, but the feeling was short lived as he watched the darkest grays and blacks also draw together creating some of the most concentrated negativity he had ever imagined. These dark mists represented events like death, fear, hatred and more.

104

He watched as one of these energies became more and more concentrated and nearly became solid and physical. It began to draw other negative mists to it, like iron filings to a magnet. The stronger it grew, the more the positive energy mists seem to dissipate in an uncontrolled chaos.

As the positive mists weakened, Theo found himself back in the physical world. Dawn was near and Theo stood in the midst of a forest. Bodies were strewn about in a most heinous way. In the middle of the apocalyptic scene stood a devilish presence. This young evil was reveling in its newly found power. Only one out of many men had managed to survive and escape. Theo knew it must have been intentional, as this evil being could have so easily destroyed this man as well.

The scene blurred and a brightness appeared that washed the colors from everything. When the brilliant light dimmed, he was now standing in the main corridor of a medical facility... the Infirmary. It was alive and bustling with medics and orderlies, inmates and visitors. He watched as the day and the people flew by in fast forward. Alongside him, he also watched the concentration of negative energy that had become a conscious entity of its own studying all of the passersby.

Theo watched in amazement and a new understanding as he saw blackish ribbons of mist leave this 'demon' and begin wrapping around and entering the bodies of the inmates and even some of the staff of the Infirmary. The beast had been weakened, but remained strong enough to retain its form and consciousness. An inmate passed by, escorted by an orderly and an attending psychiatrist. The attention of both Theo and the beast were caught by the inmate, realizing this was the same man who had been allowed to escape the forest scene. The beast let out a chuckle of the most unnerving nature and began to pursue the doctor and inmate. The doctor was quickly enveloped in the ebony monster and he stared in awe as the creature was seemingly absorbed by the unsuspecting psychiatrist.

Everything returned to fast forward mode, and escalated until the days and nights became like a flickering strobe light. When they slowed again, Theo knew that years had passed as he saw many of the same inmates and staff, but also some that were new. When time had slowed to nearly normal, it was night and he looked on as the beast left the body of the psychiatrist and began collecting his ribbons of evil as each of his hosts passed by. Their lives had spiraled over the past few years, pulled into despair and mental instability by the negativity that had been bound to them. Their expressions seemed to change in a positive way when the negativity left their bodies, but the years had taken such a toll on them that they would never recover.

The demon began to search for the man from the forest until he found his room. The beast passed straight through the door and the entirety of his evil being entered the man. The door to the man's room, though locked, burst open and the man rushed out, with a crazed look in his glowing blue eyes. Theo's spirit followed the man as his rampage was unleashed on the Infirmary. He seemed to be on a mission... a mission to destroy someone in particular, and he would not let anyone stand in his way.

Theo found himself present as the man, bare-handedly, murdered three innocent people, and he watched as the beast left the man's body and flung him out of the window as he was shot by the attending guard. He followed the entity through the wall and into the adjacent room where it had intended the final murder to occur. Inside of that room was a young woman, driven to madness by fear and grief. The beast reached for her, but was unable to physically touch her. It was a conundrum to the demon and to Theo, how this woman could remain untouchable, and yet be so obviously weak and mentally unstable.

This young woman, Madison, could feel the evil presence and had heard the commotion and gunshot in the next room. Reaching up to the neckline of her dreary gown, her fingers found the silver necklace and the moonstone pendant that hung from it. To Theo this stone glowed with an inner radiance and he could feel its power. The beast could evidently feel it too, and with a howl of displeasure, it dispersed into a hundred slivers of evil and overtook nearly the entire residence, one by one. If it could not have her, it would surround her with evil and make her life a living hell until it found a way to end her and take over her soul.

Theo reached out to Madison, but she cowered away, which astounded him. How could she possibly see him? They were existing in different times and dimensions.

"It is mine." She wept quietly, clinging to the pendant around her neck. "It was a gift... she gave it to me... when I'm dead, I will return it to her."

"Can you hear me? Can you see me?" was all that Theo could manage to get out, but there was no answer. He placed his hand on her reluctant shoulder and was given a vision within a vision... a flash back through time.

Madison was just a child of eleven or twelve. She sat crying, frightened that her parents and the church would find out that she had been able to see ghosts and spirits, as long as she could remember. They had only just moved to this small town to avoid persecution after she had been called out for her oddities in their home town. In their eyes she would be labeled as a devil worshiper or a witch, and be an outcast, or even killed for something that she had no control over. Theo thought of how cruel the people in this world could be, and it hadn't changed. People were persecuted for the color of their skin, their sexual orientation, and even their appearance; none of which is truly in their control. When narrow-minded people had influence over others, the ignorance and intolerance only grew.

He watched as a little blonde headed girl, a year or two younger than Madison walked past him and approached the crying girl. The girl's clothes were dirty and disheveled. Her bare feet gave the impression that she rarely wore shoes, and perhaps didn't even own any. In spite of her desperate appearance, she held her closed hand out to Madison.

"Here, take this. I think it's magic... maybe it can protect you." The tiny voice said.

"It's beautiful..." Madison choked out as she took a silver

necklace from the girl. The white moonstone pendant glistened in the sunlight and a rainbow of colors appeared. It truly did feel as if it held some power of good, as if it were infused with some white magic.

"The preacher man had it blessed when my momma died, and father said it would protect me. I wore it for a little while, but I think it made him sad. I think it made him think of mama, so I hid it away and told him I lost it. I got a good beatin' for that, but it was better than seeing him so sad." The cotton topped girl said as Madison put the necklace on.

The two girls giggled and played a clapping game to a rhyme they made up as they played.

"Two little girls, So cute and nice,

Met their death, In fire and ice.

For a hundred years, They played in hell,

With tortured souls, Where angles fell.

When the dead girls cried, The living came..."

"Come on now girl. Get over here now. We gotta get home." The girl's Father appeared and stopped the song short.

"I have to go." The blonde girl's eyes grew open wide as Madison hid the treasured necklace.

"Thank you for your kindness." Madison said. "I will cherish it, and I will cherish you, friend. What is your name?"

The little girl looked over her shoulder to Theo, her icy blue eyes pierced his soul in a moment of clarity. She turned back to young Madison and said, "I am Ashley, but you can call me Ash."

"I am pleased to make your acquaintance, Ash. My name is..."

Before she could finish her sentence, Theo felt himself being

108

pulled through time and space calling out "Noooooooooo!" knowing there were more pieces to the puzzle he could have discovered if he had only been able to stay in that dream world. He felt his world shaking, and was awakened by Hilary, shaking his shoulder.

"Hey buddy, time to wake up. I'm making some breakfast." She said to Theo, who rubbed his eyes, returning to reality.

Hilary

Of the four of us, Hilary was the only one who had any difficulty falling asleep. To avoid tossing and turning and possibly waking Mike, she headed downstairs to the kitchen and snatched a cold bottle of beer from the fridge. Taking the beer and her cigarettes outside, she took a seat on one of the loungers on the rear deck. Her home was just a few miles from the infirmary, but the drizzling rain had missed it. With a grinding snap, her Bic took flame and with a deep draw, she lit her cigarette. Holding it between her lips, she laid her lighter on the table next to her and with a grunt and a twist, her beer was opened.

The air was crisp and cool, but still noticeably warmer than it had been inside the old Infirmary. She sipped at her beer, thinking she wouldn't have to worry about it getting warm. The thought gave her a chill, but also made her smile as she took another deep drag and the smoke billowed from her shivering lips. While she slowly drank her beer, the night air caused her necklace to grow cold. She took it in her hand and crushed out her cigarette with the other hand.

Pulling the necklace over her head, she looked at it in the dim dusk-to-dawn light that filtered over from the front side of her home. It was a beautiful stone pendulum on a leather cord. Hilary had used it at times to connect with the spiritual world, but after tonight, her desire to be close to the other side was shaken. Placing the pendulum carefully on the table next to the half empty beer, she gazed up to the sky watching the clouds part and reveal a few brilliant stars. She took it as a sign that she should not abandon her passion and her gift. Hilary had been able to, at times, see and communicate with those who had passed.

While she watched the stars, she drifted off for a while. Her sleep, unsurprisingly, turned to dreams. Similar to Theo, she found herself inside of the Infirmary when it was still young and filled with life, twisted and tormented as it may have been. It was late evening, and many people passed by her in the hallways. None seemed to hold any special significance to Hilary until two male orderlies rushed by, their arms interlocking on either side with the arms of a young woman with coal black hair... Madison. Though no one seemed to pay notice to Hilary's presence, the two orderlies looked directly at her with eyes as cold and pale blue as the moonlight on the snow just outside the windows.

She followed them through the fourth floor of the infirmary and watched as they dragged her, against her will into the bathing therapy room. The men stripped the gown from her pale body, and forcefully picked her up and dunked her naked body into a large steel tub of icy water, going so far as to even push her head completely under the water while she struggled. Gasping as her face broke the surface of the water, the men cackled and dunked her once again. Her struggling and screaming combined with the icy waters drained her energy. When the men pulled her from the tub, she shivered and collapsed onto the floor. One of the men picked her up by grabbing her around her waist and placed her on a table against the far wall of the room. While the other man held the door closed, the first had his way with young Madison, sexually assaulting her in a very unpleasant and degrading way.

When he had finished, the men picked her completely up, and dunked her several times in a scalding hot tub of water just next to the ice bath. The second man took his turn, raping the poor girl, and while she was nearly lifeless from spending all of her energy, Hilary could feel the horrors of emotion that filled her mind. Madison could not believe this was happening to her, or that this was what her life had become. Maddie's emotions were as clear to Hilary as if she could read her mind, and Maddie was feeling that somehow she had deserved this treatment, and maybe worse.

Unable to look away, Hilary watched as the ritual abuse and

110

the 'hot and cold therapy' were repeated until the woman was all but dead. When they had finished, the cruelty continued. One of the men grabbed her gown and was about to begin dressing her when an evil grin grew across his face, exposing his crooked and yellowed teeth. He dunked the gown into the icy tub and the slid it over her dripping and tangled hair. They pulled her arms through the sleeve holes and proceeded to walk her, stumbling, back to her fourth floor apartment, where she was locked in for the night.

Hilary entered the room and watched as the men threw her to the floor and left her there, soaking wet. They grabbed up the blanket and locked the door behind them. Their voices and footsteps trailed off down the hall. Hilary wanted to comfort the poor girl, but was merely an observer from a different plane of existence. Maddie was weak and used up, but she managed to drag herself into the bed. A metallic rattle and accompanying squeaking groan came from a small radiant heater near the window and filled the small room.

Hilary began to see Maddie's breath as the room grew colder. The young woman shivered uncontrollably and curled her soaking wet body into a fetal position. Hilary found herself outside, peering in through the fourth story window. She could see the sheet beneath Madison beginning to soak through as the window began to frost over from the inside. When she could see nothing but frost through the glass, she was jolted to reality.

Nearly two hours had passed and she was nearly freezing, having fallen asleep in the deck chair. Rubbing the sleep from her eyes and rubbing warmth into her exposed arms, she rushed to the warm refuge of her home and slipped quietly back into bed for a few more hours of dreamless sleep.

Mike

Having worked that day, Mike fell into a sound sleep the moment his head hit the pillow, but like the rest of us, his sleep was plagued with unsettling dreams. As a rule, it was quite unusual for Mike to have otherworldly revelations and dreams, but this night would prove to be the exception, and not the rule.

The sunlight filtered through the thick, light gray, winter clouds. A frozen mist hung heavy in the air and shrouded the world in mystery. Mike stood outside of the infirmary, on this cold and snowy morning, watching as two men were digging feverishly into the frozen ground. Standing beside where the men dug, was a ghastly apparition of a woman with raven black hair, knotted and tangled. Bits of flesh ripped from her exposed body, leaving reddish-blackened splotches scattered about her left side. Hollow black eyes exuded sadness. Looking on, he watched as the men stopped using the shovels and began to dig at the earth with garden rakes and eventually with glove covered hands.

The ghostly woman faded into the mist, disappearing altogether. He watched as the men pulled a body, wrapped in mud stained sheets, from the ground and carried it to a nearby horse drawn wagon. Thick leather straps with black iron connecting rings and embellishments harnessed the two brown and white steeds to the black, short-sided wagon. The apparition materialized on the far side of the horses, just as the men heaved the cadaver into the back of the cart. The horses began to snort and stomp the ground wildly, as if they had been spooked by a snake, cougar, or some other predator. The two men grabbed the reins and tried to calm the horses. One of the men passed right through the ghastly form of the woman, and her form faded again, seemingly becoming wisps of fog in the breeze. A calm came over the horses and they quieted their spirits.

One of the young men scaled the side of the wagon and sat, flat legged, next to the lifeless corpse. Mounting the driver's seat, the other man took the reins in his hands, tipped his hat toward the Infirmary, and popped the horses on their hind quarters with the leather straps, making a "click-click" sound with his mouth. The horses started off very slowly down the Infirmary drive and made a nearly hairpin left turn onto the main road. Another tap with the reigns and the team broke into a slow trot.

Unexpectedly, just before they vanished out of sight, the nightmarish specter of the woman appeared on the road directly in front of the horses. The iron-shod hooves dug deep into the frozen road, stopping so abruptly that the strong snap-rings broke free from the wooden connecting shafts, allowing the wagon to roll forcefully into the rear of the horses. Now terrified, the horses reared up and twisted wildly, bucking and kicking in a frantic frenzy. The rear hooves of one horse kicked upward on the wagon, tipping it backward. The young man and the bedraggled corpse banged against the end gate, busting through it. The man tumbled hard onto the road slamming his head hard against its surface. The weathered wrappings tore free and the cadaver pummeled onto the young man, as the desiccated face and black tangled hair of the corpse slammed into him, face to morbid face.

The splintered harness shaft dug into the side of the other mare, painfully tearing its flesh, and caused it to bolt deliriously. In the chaos of the moment, the ankle of the driver had become tangled in the leather strap of the reins. Screaming feverishly, the driver was dragged nearly a mile down the road, until his boot finally came off freeing him from the torturous ride.

The man from the back of the wagon, the rider, yelled out, throwing the decomposing body from on top of him, and scuffling to his feet, he shook all over, as if he could shake the death and fear from him. He watched as his friend, the driver, was brutally dragged down the snow covered roadway. His first instinct was to run after him, to help his friend, but he had only taken a few steps when, suddenly, a dark fog rolled out from the infirmary, and surrounded the rider, whirling around him like a dust-devil of black ribbons. His focus immediately shifted to the cadaver lying, sprawled out, in the middle of the road and he was mindlessly driven to it.

Moving in a trance-like state, he trudged over to the body. Grabbing the woman's leg, he drug her off of the road, and into the drainage ditch, filled with pale shoots of long dead winter wheat and weeds, and driven snow. He rolled her corpse into the lowest part of the ditch, and nearly animalistic, began to scratch and claw at the drifted snow, covering her body entirely from sight. His energy nearly spent, he crawled back to the road and collapsed, as the swirling ribbons of dark

113

fog retreated back to the Infirmary, having served their cruel purpose. Mike watched as the rider lay there, and just beyond, the apparition of the woman appeared in the ditch, standing next to her own snow covered cadaver. It was a fair distance, but Mike could feel her pain and sorrow, and even thought this spirit seemed to be crying, and calling out for attention and help, with arms outstretched. While he gazed directly at her, the snow began to fall harder, with more and bigger flakes, until the scene had become a near white out.

"Mike... you awake?" A voice called and he was shaken back to reality.

"Huh? Yeah... I guess so." He grumbled still half asleep.

"You hungry?" The voice was now easily recognized as his wife, Hilary. "I'm going to cook breakfast for everybody."

"Yeah, sure... give me a minute to wake up and get dressed." He said, rubbing his eyes and wanting to pull the covers over his head.

"If it's cold when you come down, it's your own fault... I tried to get you up." Hilary nudged at him.

"I'm coming." He said, less groggy, but more grumpy. "Hey!... I gotta tell you about this freaky dream I had last night."

"Oh yeah?" Hilary looked at him curiously. "I had a bad dream last night too. What was yours about?"

"Not right now...remind me later and I'll tell you all about it. Man was it messed up." He said sitting up on the edge of the bed and throwing the covers off. Mike drew in a deep breath through his nose and smelled a heavenly aroma. "Coffee?"

"I already have a pot brewing" Hilary smiled as she passed through the doorway and turned to head down the stairs to the kitchen. "There might be a cup left, if you come down quick enough."

***

I was drawn to the kitchen by the metallic clatter of pans as Hilary began to prepare breakfast. Soon the popping sound of bacon and its salty, smoky aroma filled the room. The scents and sounds of a long overdue meal had aroused Theo as well. Sleepy eyed, Mike, Theo, and I gathered around the oak dining table. Hilary laid out a serving bowl of biscuits, a plate full of bacon, and served up scrambled eggs onto each plate. The aroma was heavenly, and the scent of slightly stronger than normal coffee topped off the perfect meal to awaken to.

After a few mumbled, yet heartfelt 'Thank you's, the table went silent, except for the clinking sound of forks on plates, slurping coffees and moans of delight.. Our mouths and bellies were stuffed with a morning feast we hadn't expected, but so desperately needed. About half way through the meal, Hilary broke the silence.

"So, what about that 'freaky dream' you had Mike?" She said, glancing sideways at him and taking another bite from one of her bacon strips.

"Oh yeah...I almost forgot." A look of being deep in thought came over his face. "Huh..."

"Go on, I want to hear this." I coaxed him on, wondering if he had a similar dream to mine. I didn't plan on sharing my dream, but I was curious about his.

"Strange..." He said slowly, racking his brain to remember.

"Well... was it about the infirmary?" Hilary finally asked. I caught Theo's head jerk toward Hilary as she mentioned it, and then turn straight away to Mike.

"Well, hell! I can't remember." Mike's frustration was obvious. "I don't think it was about the infirmary, but I just can't freakin' remember." He took a few more bites. "All I remember is that it was so real, and so weird. Damn... well, if I remember it, I'll let you know."

We finished up the meal, not leaving any left overs whatsoever. We helped clear the table as Hilary rinsed the dishes and loaded the dishwasher, while Mike started a second pot of coffee. We all enjoyed a second round of java while we rehashed the night's events.

We packed up and loaded Theo's car and with hugs and handshakes, said our farewells. The ride home was quieter than I had expected, but even after a few hours of sleep, we were still spent. The hours in the car dragged on, as I watched the fields and trees zipping past the passenger window. Well over half way home, Theo pulled into a rest stop.

"Are you okay to drive?" He asked. "Staring down the highway is making me a zombie."

"I'm fine to drive the rest of the way. I dozed for a while already." I wasn't being perfectly honest. I had closed my eyes for an hour or more though I hadn't actually fallen asleep.

Soon we were entering the Evansville city limits, and I was looking forward to being home. I pulled Theo's little silver-blue Subaru into a parking space in front of my apartment. I gave Theo a nudge, quietly waking him before I opened the trunk. I unlocked my apartment door and closing the door behind me, exited through the sliding glass door, leaving it open. Theo was already pulling the silver trimmed, black equipment cases from the trunk and helped carry them into the apartment.

"Where do you want them?" He asked, his voice still groggy.

"Right here." I answered, pointing to the floor just inside of the sliding door. Theo gave an unsure look. "Later... I'll put 'em away later. I'm just glad to be home." I looked around at the familiar surroundings. "You'd better get on the road and get yourself home... and thanks for everything."

Theo's eyes squinted nearly closed and he smiled through his exhaustion. "Welcome... Thanks for inviting me along."

"Anytime." I said, as I waved good-bye.

I still found it refreshing that he openly appreciated being part of the team. So many (not that there had been that many) of our temporary team members felt like they were 'god's gift to the paranormal' and we were lucky to have them on our team. I quickly put an end to those, and kept only the most humble and brilliant, open minds. I never made it past the living room. My shoes came off, and my butt hit the comfy cushions of the couch. I sat there for most of the rest of the day, contemplating everything from the cave-in that nearly cost me everything, to the curious, nightmarish dream.

My son Daniel came home, just as the sun began to sink into the horizon, and the sky became faded from blue to purple and then countless shades of orange and red. He, too, was worn-out after a weekend staying up late playing video games and getting up early to play football with his friends. After a short father and son talk about our weekends, he disappeared into his room and never even turned on the light. While I was motivated enough to stand, I decided to take a long, hot shower and wash away the weight of the investigation. As I disrobed, the sound of sand and debris fell to the tile floor of the bathroom, reminding me how badly I needed this shower. The scent of my body wash was more refreshing than expected. As I lathered up my scrubby and began to scour away the dust that I didn't even realize I had acquired, the warmth of the cascading water began to work its magic and loosen up the tension of my shoulders, back, and literally every muscle of my body. When my shower ended, I stepped onto the bath mat, wrapped a towel around my waist and opened the door, letting the steam pour out. I toweled off, slipped into a pair of comfy boxers, and melted into my bed... with hopes of dreamless sleep.

Photo by Rick Kueber

CHAPTER 9
THE SOUNDS OF SILENCE

The week progressed as most do, with days filled with work and school, and evenings of dinner, homework, and a little veg time in front of the television. When Thursday rolled around, I decided to contact the team to try to set up a time to review the audio and photos from the Infirmary investigation. I directed a text to Theo, Katie, and Jenn.

'We need to get together. We have some audio and lots of photos to review. Any free time this weekend?' -EVPRick

'afternoons are best for me' -EVP Theo

'I'm off this weekend, so just let me know when. WOO HOO!' -EVP Jenn

'I work saturday til noon. :(' -EVP Kate

'How about saturday at 2?' -EVPRick

'Actually, how about 1? I already have a sitter, so I can come straight from work.' -EVP Kate

All agreed and the time was set. I went about the rest of my evening doing the mundane chores of everyday life; cooking, doing dishes, laundry... but I was also able to spend time with my son, which was a blessing. The following day flew by and soon I was home for the weekend. Daniel and I went out to eat at his favorite buffet and then stopped by the corner video box to rent the latest scary DVD release. We stopped for candy... Twizzlers Pull-n-Peel for him, and Good-n-Plentys for me. It was a man's night at home. The lights were off, the surround sound was on, and we munched our way through the creepy movie. Daniel and I would look at each other and smile or laugh every chance we got. I knew it made watching the DVD less frightening, even though he loved scary movies, he didn't care much for sleeping after watching one. Ah, the joys of parenthood... nothing was more fulfilling that being there for my son, through all of the fun, the frights, and even the sad times. We had a bond that I prayed would never weaken, but I knew he would soon be entering high school, and those years would be difficult. How difficult, I could not even imagine. So for now, I relished in the good times... the times when he still needed and wanted his dad around.

Midday was approaching on Saturday, and my son was still sleeping, a sure sign he was a teenager. I opened up the make-shift office and fired up the computers. While I waited, I was intently focused on loading the photos into two of the computers, and putting the audio files on the other computer and my laptop. My phone buzzed in my pocket, startling me. It was Jenn and my first fear was that she was going to have to cancel.

"Hey Jenn, what's up?" I answered cheerily.

"Weeell..." Her stretched out word immediately had me concerned. "...I'm actually running a bit early. Is it okay if I go ahead and come over?"

"Yeah, that'd be fine." The relief was probably obvious to her, but I didn't care. She already knew how much I valued her as a friend and teammate.

"Good." She half groaned and exhaled loudly. "...'cause I'm

pulling in now."

I jumped to attention, rushing to pull Daniel's door shut quietly, and then threw a dish towel over the dishes in the sink. I methodically moved on to the living room to snatch up the empty soda cans and candy packages and rush them to the already full trash can... such is the life of this single parent/bachelor. There was a tap at the sliding glass door, and I gave the apartment a once-over glance before I opened the vertical blinds and opened the door, welcoming one of my best friends into my home.

"Hey girl!" I joked.

"Hey there E-V-Prick. How ya been?" Her tone was surprisingly up, as she stepped up into the bachelor pad, and without hesitation gave me a big hug, and a pat on the shoulder.

"Not been too bad... livin' the dream.. ya know." I was good at always putting on a good front to hide my true feelings. If I were going to be perfectly honest, I would have said, 'This case is so strange, it has me freaked the hell out, and I'm scared to death that I am going to fail as a parent... oh, and I think I'm falling in love with the most beautiful woman I have ever met, who has clearly placed me into the permanent friend zone.', but I just smiled instead. "You want something to drink?"

"Got it." She said, sitting her bag on the couch and pulling out a 20 oz. Dr. Pepper.

"Okay... I'm gonna grab a Dew. You want to go ahead and start looking through the photos?" I asked as I headed into the small apartment sized kitchen, intentionally leaving the light off to hide the disarray.

"Duh! I'm dying to see the Infirmary!" She poked her head around the corner, into the kitchen. "No pun intended."

"I kinda thought you'd say that, but maybe we should wait for Katie and Theo." I said, knowing exactly how she would react. She poked her head around the corner again, and stuck her tongue out at me making a sour face at me. "Jenn, you never disappoint."

I followed her into the office and sat down at one of the computers that I had loaded the photos into. Motioning to her, she pulled a chair up next to mine. I wiggled the mouse on the desktop and the screen saver disappeared, revealing the first full screen photo of the exterior of the Infirmary. It had a blueish cast from the metal-halide light in the parking lot, but was eerily beautiful. Jenn gasped.

"Shut up! I missed that?" She said wide eyed and open mouthed.

"You had good reason." I quickly became uncomfortable. "I'm sorry. I should have asked... how are you?"

"Ugh..." She rolled her eyes and my heart sank, anticipating the worst. "I got called in early in for a follow up visit yesterday."
In my mind I was saying 'AND?!?!?!' but on the outside, I just sat there quietly and waited for her to be ready to tell me. I expected the worst, but prayed for the best.

"Well, my dumb ass doctor thought my lymphoma was back, but I just had a few inflamed lymph nodes. I'm fighting off an infection, a cold or something, and I'm on antibiotics, but I'm fine." I could hear the mixed emotions of frustration and relief in her words. Personally, I felt like every muscle in my body relaxed all at once.

"That's fantastic news!" My voice nearly failed me, as the words trembled. I almost teared up, and to keep her from seeing, I was the one who jumped up and gave her a big hug.

"Now, back to these pictures." She quickly changed the subject, which was perfectly fine with me. "I am so pissed that I missed out because of a misdiagnosis... you think I could sue for malpractice or something? I mean, I am definitely experiencing some pain and suffering right now."

"I kinda doubt it, but hey, call an ambulance chaser and see what they think." I almost laughed, which was refreshing. I clicked on the arrow button and moved it to the next photo just as a "Bang-bang-bang" came at the door. Jenn and I both jumped and I stood up.

"Well, check this one out while I get the door." I instructed her and disappeared into the other room.

Jenn scanned over the second photo of the Infirmary, taken from the rear corner of the building. After a minute of looking it over carefully, she zoomed in and started scanning it meticulously, bit by bit. As I appeared in the doorway, she quickly zoomed back out and turned to see Theo and Katie following close behind. Jenn popped up to pass out her usual hugs and hellos. She went through the story of the misdiagnosis again and they were as thrilled at the news as I had been. Eventually we had all taken seats and the topic turned to the Infirmary investigation.

"Check this crap out Katie." Jenn said snidely, clicking the back arrow to show the first photo of the entire front of the building.

"No flippin' way! You aren't serious, are you?" Kate exasperated.

"Dead serious." Theo chuckled with a grin.

"I can't believe I couldn't go." Katie expressed her displeasure. "Are we going back?"

"Yeah, I'm sure we will have to go back. That place is seriously messed up.. and by messed up, I mean it's freakin' crawling with ghosts." I certainly had every intention of returning as soon as possible.

"That place is haunted as hell!" Theo wasn't really trying to be funny, or ironic. He was being honest. There seemed to be countless tormented souls within the walls of the old structure, and at least one evil force that could easily be labeled as demonic.

"Take a look at this one." Jenn said as she moved to the second photo and we all looked at the rear of the building. I was studying it pretty closely, but didn't see anything spectacular about it. I thought, perhaps, she was just showing the other view to Katie.

"Yep... I'm jealous." Katie said. "That place looks amazing."

"Look closer." Jenn coaxed us, and we stared at it in depth. The four of us leaning closer and closer to the screen until our heads almost bumped into each other. "Well, hell, I have to point it out to you, I guess." She pointed to a fourth story window and then with a click of the mouse, zoomed in close.

"A face!" I blurted out.

"It's a woman!" Katie added all aflutter.

"Hmmm..." Theo thought out loud. "You think it's her? Maddie?"

"Hard to say, with all of the spirits we encountered there, but whoever it is, it looks like they were waiting for us." I was being as honest as I could be. Aside from a dream-vision that I could not entirely trust, I had no real idea of what Madison looked like.

"Well, here is how I have it set up... those two computers have the photos on them, and this one and my laptop have the audio files on them. So, who wants what?" I was excited to get started, but the girls were more interested in hearing about the investigation before beginning the review. Theo and I told our stories, from our sighting of the bald eagle to our return trip home, adding details to each other's tales and filling in bits that the other had left out. Jenn and Katie were nearly speechless when we had finished, and other than asking questions throughout our narratives, the only thing really said at the end of our recants was from Katie and obviously seconded by Jenn.

"So, when do we go back? I'll hire a visiting nurse if the boys get sick next time. I'm not missing out on this place again."

"Soon, I hope." I answered. "Let me know when you all have another open weekend... of course, it's going to be unbearably cold soon."

"True." Theo agreed. "This is Bangs... Northern Ohio. The winters are brutal."

124

"Right... and with all of the holiday stuff coming up, it's gonna be hard to get all four of us free on the same weekend." Jenn added.

"Five." I corrected her and got a few sideways looks. "Hilary makes five, and we can't very well go without her." The nods let me know they all understood what I was getting at. It looked like late winter, early spring was our best bet for a return to the Infirmary.

"Okay then, let's get to it. I'll take this one." Katie said tilting her head towards the computer nearest her and sliding on a pair of headphones. She used the mouse to click the play button and leaned her chin on her hands. I took the laptop and the other audio review, while Theo and Jenn began searching through the photos, talking back and forth and pointing to one another's screen. At first it was distracting, because I wanted to know what they were looking at, what they were seeing, but when I looked over to Katie, she had her back completely turned to them and was intently listening, staring at the screen, and occasionally stopping to replay a section a few times before moving on. I followed her lead and turned my back to them.

I did my best to ignore Jenn and Theo feverishly scanning the photos, jotting down notes and numbers in a note pad and chattering about their findings, but I caught myself periodically glancing over my shoulder. It seemed apparent to me that they were on to something, and the anticipation was almost more than I could bear.

The endless static, and eardrum shattering scuffling noises were interspersed with typical e.v.p. questions and bits of conversations between Theo, Hilary, Mike and I. I was about to give my ears and my sanity a break from the noise when something grabbed my attention. My head snapped back to the screen as I paused the recording. I slid the play-bar back about a minute and listened again, watching the screen intently. I noted the time marker where the anomaly occurred and paused it again. I wrote down the precise moment of the recording as e.v.p. #1 on my notebook and selected a few seconds before to a few seconds after. I looped the selected audio and pressed the play button, listening over and over again. The anomaly was actually a disembodied voice which

125

occurred just as Hilary and I were discussing the incredible drop in temperature on the fourth floor of the Infirmary. I scratched down my first assumption of what it said.

- Kill him... something

I stopped the loop and slid my headphones off slowly and indiscreetly looked to Katie out of the corner of my eye, but it was all for naught. She had already stopped her recording and was turned toward me, staring blankly, and waiting.

"What?" She said bluntly, which caught everyone's attention.

"Pretty sure I have something here." I said as my eyes passed from one teammate to another.

"Let me check it out." Katie said reaching out her hand.

"Okay. I have an idea of what it's saying, but I can't make it all out." These words pulled groans and whines from Theo and Jenn, disappointed that Katie was given first listen. She put the headphones in place, cupped her hands over them, holding them in place and nodded for me to play the clip.

"Whaaa?" She said loudly, forgetting that we could hear her. She looked at me with wide eyes and spun her hand and pointer finger in a circular motion, which was EVP code for: 'Play it again'. She repeated this several times before jotting a note on her paper and removing the headphones.

"Okay... what the hell? We wanna hear too." Jenn pouted, voicing her evident impatience.

"I was just about the same place, but I didn't hear that at all. What did you think it said?" Katie asked, while I unwrapped the p.c. speaker cord and swapped it for the headphones.

"I couldn't make it all out, but it sounded like three words..." I began to doubt my own ears. "I though it said 'Kill him...something' but I'm not sure." I slid my notebook over to show what I had written down.

126

"That's a little creepy." Theo said, flashing back to the collapse that could have easily killed me.

"That's not exactly what I heard." Katie said sheepishly. I felt overly paranoid that maybe I was imagining things. "It sounds more like 'Kill them all' to me."

"Aw hell, I gotta hear this!" Jenn couldn't hide her excitement, which sort of bothered me.

"Really Jenn? I mean, I know you weren't there, but this is a voice that was talking about killing us... don't you find that a little grim?" I couldn't contain my displeasure at her bubbly exhilaration.

"I'm not thrilled about *that*... It's just that there seems to be an intelligent, although malevolent, haunting." She backpedaled well. "Besides... you know how much I love hearing any voice phenomenon."

With the speaker hooked up, I raised the volume and pushed the play button several times so everyone could hear. It now seemed much clearer than before... Katie was right. "Kill them all." The voice was male, deep and raspy. It was also painfully forceful. It seemed to be giving instruction, and that thought sent my mind whirling in a thousand different terrifying directions.

"Yeah..." Theo said slowly. "Kill 'em all is what I heard. When was this?"

"It was me and Hilary on the fourth floor when it started getting really cold." I explained.

"Well that kind of an evil command would correlate with the sudden temperature drop." Theo rubbed his forehead with his eyes closed. "Isn't that about the time that all the shadows appeared?"

"Yes... it was shortly before that. And it was just when I would have sworn Hil and I were going to freeze to death." I validated his recollection.

"Right... not good." He said and everyone went quiet. I didn't know what to say besides what naturally came out.

"Okay, back to it, I guess." I swapped the speaker for the headphones and we all went back to our own worlds of evidence review.

Everyone was soon back into their reviewing and note taking when I thought I heard something else; a voice similar to the previous one, but louder, and much angrier sounding than before. I backed it up to listen one more time. Once again, I thought I had it mostly figured out, but instead of wasting time listening a hundred times, I ripped the headphones from my ears and was about to say, 'I've got something' when I noticed Katie sternly looking at her screen and listening. She was replaying something as well.

"Whatcha got?" I said, leaning over to her.

"You tell me... sounds like 'I lost'... something... 'old' maybe." She seemed pleased with her catch, although what I heard was a bit more disturbing. "You wanna hear it?"

"Already did. I stopped at the same place." My swapping of the wires drew Theo and Jenn's attention again. Once hooked up, I adjusted the volume and played the clip several times. Jenn perked up after the second time, and by the fourth time she was trying to talk over the clip, so I paused it for a moment.

"Sorry, but...not sorry." She said sarcastically. "I know what it's saying." we all listened carefully to what Jenn had to say, and I agreed with her interpretation of the ominous voice. "That's Hilary, right?... saying 'We can help you... etcetera, etcetera... and she's talking to all the shadow people, right?" I nodded in agreement. "The voice is pissed-flippin off, and says... 'MY LOST SOULS'. I think it's ticked off that you are trying to help them."

Theo dropped his head, pointed his finger at Jenn and said, "Exactly." He raised his head back up and looked me in the eye. "When I said we weren't welcome there, this is why. This being, this demon, wants to keep its control over all of those poor lost souls... that's where it gets all of its power."

128

"Wow... yeah... that makes sense." My expression and my tone were flat. "We have to find a way to help them."

Our conversation bounced back and forth from cleansing rituals to sage smudging and even calling in the clergy. We discussed what order we might try what ideas, and whether or not we would be able to help all of them, or any of them. Before long we were rambling on until we were finally quieted by Jenn.

"So, are we gonna finish this up?" She broke our wandering communication. "I'm gonna be getting hungry before long."

With very little else said, we turned back to our tasks at hand. Time passed quickly, and though Katie and I both thought we had several other e.v.p.s, when it came down to it we dismissed or debunked all but one other e.v.p. This last voice that we caught on our audio recording was different and caught just as we decided to call it a night. The other voice had been strong, evil, overpowering and male. This e.v.p. was clearly heard by all without question as to what was said. It was desperate, distraught, female, and echoed something Hilary had conveyed to me from her dreams. This was two distinct sentences, simply saying, "I'm lost." and "Don't leave me here."

We recapped all of the clipped e.v.p.s captured and I saved them to a flash drive to send to Hilary and Mike.

"So, what did you two find?" I finally asked Jenn and Theo.

"Well now... this is interesting, but I can't say for sure what it is." Jenn started.

"Whatever it is, it seems to have been following you around from the fourth floor, before and after the collapse, and followed us until we left the building." Theo explained what we were about to see.

"You see this here?" Jenn asked as she pulled up the first of many pictures and pointed to a gray mist that covered a corner of the picture. "Any idea what that is?"

"Maybe my breath? It was cold." I tried my best to debunk the vapor.

"That was my first thought too, but then I realized it wasn't in the first pictures, but once it showed up, it stayed until you started taking pics outside just before we left." Theo argued. "And then there's this..."

I watched as Jenn stopped on about the fifth picture where the mist seemed to be right behind Theo, who was actually standing about fifteen foot in front of the camera. It wasn't his breath, because it was behind him, and it wasn't my breath because Theo was between the mist and where I took the photo. It would have been a conundrum to most, but we already knew how actively haunted the Infirmary was, so it wasn't so much what was in the photos, but who. We continued to look through the rest of the photos and when we had finished, we looked them over again and again. The hair stood up on the back of my neck each time the next picture popped up. I knew how closely we were being watched and followed, and with the recorded voices, we felt pretty certain of its intent.

"You can take this for what you want, lens flare, infra-red reflection, or whatever, but these photos were all taken on the fourth floor." Theo explained as he pulled up the first of several photos. "You see here? This orangey dot... it's like something is pointing out items or places of importance or significance."

"Isn't that just outside of Maddie's room?" I asked.

"Yes." Theo answered as he moved to the next photo. "...and this is in Maddie's room. See the squiggly orange light over her bed?"

"That's crazy!" Katie added. "Why orange?"

"You think Ash followed you there?" Jenn asked inquisitively.

"Hmmm... I don't know, but I suppose it is possible, or maybe it's Maddie trying to lead us somewhere." I answered back.

130

"This is the last one with that light in it." Theo revealed the last photo.

"I knew it!" I shouted. "Sorry, but I just knew that had significance." The final photo showed the same light focused directly on the chest of drawers I so desperately wanted to explore, and this photo was taken after the collapse. I couldn't help but feel that somehow, some way, I had to get into that last drawer.

I loaded the photos onto the flash drive in the order they were taken and I renamed the photos as 'mist 1', 'mist 2', 'light 1', 'light 2', etc. I had decided to email the files to Hilary and save the flash drive for team use. Everyone helped power down the computers and was about to leave when I made a suggestion.

"How about going out for a bite?" I smiled. "Hacienda is just around the corner."

"Mmmm... that sounds great." Jenn closed her eyes in food ecstasy.

"I could go for something." Theo agreed.

"Quesadillas, here I come!" Katie said, being her typical goofy self.

We drove to Hacienda separately and once seated, we ordered drinks, and eventually food. The chips and salsa that they were so famous for were virtually devoured within minutes of arriving. We spoke about the haunting evidence we had captured and of the upcoming investigation, whenever that may be. We also talked about our everyday lives and things more uplifting. Before long, some of us were on our second drink (mine was, of course Crown Royal & Coke) and we had begun to laugh and the heaviness of the investigation was temporarily left behind. It was just then that something came up that I neither expected, or was ready for.

"So have you seen Tabitha lately? She hasn't been around the bookstore much." Theo looked to me.

131

"You two are becoming quite an item, huh?" Katie teased, raising her eyebrows.

"Uh... not really... I mean, we have become very good friends, but we aren't an item... Just ask her, she'll tell you." I winked at my team, denying the truth, that I had hoped and wished that we would be more than friends.

I tried to stay in the present, but my mind wandered to the few meetings with Tabitha over coffee, dinner, or just hanging out together to watch a DVD. I later thought that there was some irony to the fact that the ghosts of an infirmary from more than a hundred years in the past, that so many of us had dreamed about were replaced by the ghost of a relationship in my head that only existed in my dreams. When we had finished up our meal, and our tongues grew tired, we shook hands, or waved, or hugged good-bye and I returned to the apartment where my son had donned his headphones and was playing his favorite video game with his on-line friends. I retreated to the solitude of my room, and spent the evening alone with my thoughts, my dreams, and my aspirations.

The next morning I met Tabitha for a cup of coffee, and we talked about all sorts of things from work to the Ohio trip and her new endeavor, a natural and healing stone Jewelry business called Cherished Elements. We enjoyed our time together, but I evaded the one thing I had promised myself I would say. I could not bring myself to risk losing our friendship and decided to keep my feelings to myself, at least for the time being.

Photos by Rick Kueber

Photos by Rick Kueber

CHAPTER 10

WINTER

Halloween decorations had been put away, and replaced by the colors of fall, pilgrims, turkeys, and cornucopias. Thanksgiving was soon upon us, and my heart broke, thinking that I would be making a meager meal that my son wouldn't even want to eat (except for turkey and croissants). A Thanksgiving feast for two was not only depressing, but it also made me think of how different it would be from all of his Thanksgivings of the past. There were always huge meals and literally dozens of family and friends gathered together being thankful for each other. Only a few days before the holiday, I received a text message from Tabitha.

"Hey... do you want to come to my parents house for Thanksgiving?" -Tab

"Really? I'd love to come, honestly, but my son would be coming along too. Are you sure it's ok?" -Rick

"Of course. My mom actually suggested it. We'll be eating at 2." -Tab

"Wow.. that sounds great. Thank you... you sure you are ok with this?"   -Rick

"Wouldn't have invited you if I wasn't. Lol !" -Tab

"True. Should I bring anything? And where do they live?"   -Rick

"There will be plenty, so no need to bring anything....

The texts eventually ended with my thanking her once again. Even though I knew she only thought of me as a friend, I was blessed to have such a good friend whose parents would gladly open their home and share their family time with someone whom they had only met at one of the Barnes & Noble seminars that we had been involved with. A funny thought crossed my mind. The truth was that Tabitha was perfectly happy being single and independent and perhaps I was invited to keep her relatives from giving her a hard time about being single. True or not, the thought made me smile.

It was a nice Thanksgiving, and I was truly grateful for a friendship like that. The next weeks flew by, as I attempted to prepare for Christmas. My son and I attended my family Christmas get together which was always the weekend before the actual holiday. My family had grown so large, with four generations attending, that we rented out a party house at a local park. It was great to see some of my relatives that I hadn't seen since the last Christmas, and I was saddened to see the empty seats where other family members should have been sitting, but weren't. Some chose not to come, while others were no longer with us. A fire was built in the large stone fireplace, and tables were set up like a buffet and covered in more food than we could have eaten if we had been there for a week.

In the midst of our meal, when the conversation had gone quieter, my thoughts wandered back to the Infirmary. There were so many unmarked 'paupers graves' that I nearly broke into tears right there in the middle of the meal. How lonely it must have been for so many of the residents and inmates who had no one at all in their lives outside of the Infirmary's walls. Poor Madison, what must it have been like to have spent so many years with no family or real friends to share her holidays with? Such a young and troubled girl whose life was so lonely that no one ever came to visit, no one even claimed her body when she so tragically died at only twenty-five. Now, even more than a hundred years after her death, she still begged to not be left behind and forgotten.

In the week between my family get together and the actual holiday, I managed to get the entire team together for a holiday gathering at the Hacienda restaurant for a mid-afternoon meal. We sat amidst the Mexican themed surroundings, intermixed with Christmas decorations and talked about our lives, our kids, significant others, our careers, and of course, the case of the Infirmary. Most of our conversations were lighthearted and filled with laughter and sarcasm. I avoided bringing up Madison, as much as possible, but I could not control my friends' choice of conversation topics.

"So Theo, about this Maddie..." Jennifer started. "How the hell did you know we wouldn't be able to find her?"

"Just a feeling, really. I keep feeling like she has been a mixed up and lost girl for most of her life." He answered back. "So, you didn't get very far tracing her history?"

"Uh, no." Katie said bluntly.

"Bummer. I was really hoping we could find out why she had been committed to the Infirmary." I pondered the possibilities and the countless connections that we could have made, if only we could have retraced the path that led to her madness.

"Tell them what you did find though." Jenn said, looking to Katie.

"Yeah, this is so odd, it's almost creepy." A look of mystery came over her. "We searched every site, called every library, searched public and private records, as much as possible. We looked for a Madison Taylor born in the 1860's, and even into the 1850's just in case her age was not accurate. Nothing."

137

"So, it was during one of our many searches that Katie found a birth record of a Taylor E. Madison born in 1863." Jenn was bubbling, but I didn't see how this was such an interesting find.

"So, where is the odd and creepy part?" Theo interjected.

"Theo, you read my mind." I said without thinking.

"Yeah, you know... psychic..." Theo joked.

"Well the creepy part is that Taylor Madison wasn't from Ohio..." Jennifer grinned. "You ready for this?" She said, directing our attention to Katie again.

"She was born in West Virginia... in a little town near Summersville, West Virginia." Katie flailed her hands and opened her mouth open wide as if to show an exaggerated surprise.

"There may be no correlation, but why are we constantly reminded of Ash, and that home, that town..." Jenn stated the truth in the form of a question.

"I know what you mean, I still see her in my dreams. Not as many nightmares as I used to have, but she still haunts my dreams." I recalled some of the more recent and vivid dreams I had experienced, though only one of them seemed relevant to the Infirmary case.

"Me too." Theo mumbled, almost to himself. He thought back to his dream at Hilary's house, but said nothing to the team. He wasn't sure if it was a dream or a vision, or what it really meant... not yet anyway.

We talked about the findings, and lack thereof, and eventually allowed our talk to diminish back to everyday life and the simple things, such as our holiday plans. We had spent several hours in each other's company and I was thankful to have a team of such goodhearted and loyal friends.

***

I had bought a few small and simple gifts for Tabitha and had neatly tucked them into a gift bag, stuffing the top with festive tissue paper. Christmas Eve had arrived and Tabitha had asked if I was going to be home so she could drop off a Christmas goodie bag. When she stopped by, I invited her inside to warm up with a cup of freshly brewed coffee. It was bitterly cold for December in Southern Indiana, so she graciously accepted. I handed her a steaming mug and we took a seat on the couch while she thawed out. A few minutes later, she handed me her bag, and before I opened it, I handed her the gift bag I had put together. She smiled and had an odd look on her face when she saw one of the gifts was a holiday spiced coffee blend. Our friendship had started over a cup of coffee and it was my way of saying, 'I remember.'

"I know, it's not much, but I just wanted to say thanks for being my friend." I had a hard time looking her directly in the eye, feeling the presents were impersonal, though I had actually put a lot of thought into them.

"No, it's great... it's just that... well, if you open your bag... I got you the same coffee blend." Her revelation was comforting. The gift bag was filled with homemade treats and a jar of apple-butter from her mom, the coffee blend and a few other thoughtful odds and ends.

Late that night, during a text conversation, she said she was at home with her friend Jackie, wrapping Christmas gifts and I was welcome to come over too. I did just that. It was nearly midnight when I left and my son was fast asleep on the couch, so I wrote a note letting him know I was only blocks away if he needed me.

The three of us had a good time, laughed, listened to music and I let my cares melt away, even if only for a few short hours. When I was about to say my good nights to the girls and head home to pack presents quietly under the tree, Tabitha disappeared into the other room and returned with another gift for me. I opened the brightly colored paper and revealed a beautiful book with a mirror finished front cover. Engraved on it were the words, "Inspiration Sparks". Opening it I realized it was a journal to write down my deepest thoughts and secrets, and it even had a pen holder with a matching silver ink pen. I smiled and opened my arms. Hesitantly, she gave me a hug. This moment meant so much to me, not the hug as much as having someone who was such a genuine friend. My team, every one of them, were amazing friends and I couldn't have created better friends with my imagination, but we were bound together by a common passion of the paranormal and the life altering experiences that we shared. Tabitha and I had no common bond. We were just acquaintances who became friends, and that friendship had its own unique bond, that I shared with no one else.

***

New Year's Eve, Valentine's Day, and a few lesser holidays came and went, while the case of Ms. Madison Taylor stayed in the back of our minds. Aside from occasional phone calls and text messages from Hilary, which didn't always relate to the Infirmary, my team and I let the haunting remain on the back burner while the harsh winter months trudged by ever so slowly. It had been one of the most brutal winters I could ever remember. The temperatures hit record lows and stayed there for weeks at a time, while we received more ice and snow that we had in the past decade combined.

It was on a Friday night of unusual winter weather, a phenomenon that had been recently labeled as 'Thunder Snow', that a new urge to solve the case and help all of those distraught souls presented itself to me. I had opened the blinds in my bedroom, and with the lights off, I laid in my bed and watched the large and fluffy flakes drifting down from the night sky, and slowly drifted off to sleep.

The fog cleared and I found myself standing in a quarter acre of open grass, fenced in with wrought iron. It was twilight and in the far corner of the gated area, near a line of leafless trees stood two small children, a girl in a short dress and a younger boy in loose pants and a white shirt that was also too big for him. Without a word, and no gesturing, the children beckoned to me. I drifted towards them effortlessly. Closer now, I could make out the features of their faces and unique distinctions. The young boy was unfamiliar to me, but the girl...

"It is now time." The little blonde girl spoke. "You must act now."

"Ash..." My words hung heavy in my throat. "How? What do we do?"

"Introduce the pasts." Her hollow voice puzzled me.

"Pasts?" I was confounded by what she could mean.

"Each of you have a connection to our pasts..." As her words filled my ears, I felt the presence of others surrounding me. Looking left and right, I found myself surrounded by ghostly images of my teammates.

"But, I don't know this boy, or his past." My heart sunk, feeling I would not be able to help the poor souls of the haunted Infirmary.

"Cordially introduce the pasts. NOW!" Her final word seemed a combination of fury and urgency.

"But, how do we do that?" I felt that the entire team was asking this question. As the words left my mouth, the two spectral children became motionless, more transparent, and seemed frozen in time. In fact, their forms appeared to transform into pure ice, like a sculpture of the two where they stood. I started to move closer when the 'ice sculptured' children burst into flames. My background in science and physics told me this was empirically impossible, yet as the two melted away, the flames grew more intense. I felt that I was being pulled away from this mysterious scene when Ashley's voice haunted my dream one last time.

"Act quickly, act now." her voice echoed in my head. "Strangers will soon threaten them... expose them... Introduce the pasts."

With that the dream ended and I awoke to several inches of newly fallen snow blanketing the world outside. I knew I had to do something quickly, but I did not really know what. All I could think of, was to plan our return visit to the Infirmary as soon as possible, as soon as the roads were clear enough to travel with as many of my team that could

141

accompany me. First step... call the team together. Second step... call Hilary.

I actually called my three amigos instead of texting them and we agreed that if the roads were clear enough, we would meet up on Sunday around noon at the Starbucks inside the local Barnes & Nobles as we had always done in the past. I sent Hilary a social media message asking if she would be available for a Skype call at noon on Sunday. It was hours later when my phone lit up with her response. I logged into the social media app on my iphone and checked the message.

"Sorry, I was working at the spa today. Yeah, I'll be around Sunday. Just call, and I'll answer, or call you right back." - Hil

"Great. Talk to you then." - Rick

Saturday proved to be a decent winter day; cold and snow covered, but sunny. The high reached into the twenties, which was warmer that it had been in days. By this time of year, mid-March, it was usually averaging temperatures well above freezing. The sun, the temps above twenty and the solution that had been sprayed on the streets helped to melt away most of the snow that covered the roads, leaving only a few slick spots. So, as it turned out, we were all able to meet up as planned.

I awoke early on Sunday morning, got my shower, and prepared for my day. I donned a set of lightweight thermal underwear, just in case the roads were worse than expected, I became stranded and had to walk to the book store, or home. I snacked on a microwave ready sausage biscuit from the freezer and gathered up a notebook, pen, my laptop and a digital recorder. I paused in the living room where my son had fallen asleep on the couch watching television the night before. I stood next to him, looking on while he lay there in peaceful slumber. I gently rubbed his shoulder and he opened one eye, looking up at me.

"I'm going up to the bookstore for coffee with Theo, Jenn and Katie. I won't be gone long." I whispered. "You want anything while I'm out?"

"Cappuccino..." His voice was hoarse from sleep. He only uttered the one word before closing his eye to dose back off.

"Okay buddy. I'll bring you one back." I said softly not knowing if he was awake enough to even hear me. "Love you buddy." I muttered with a smile as I closed the front door and locked it behind me.

I had to scrape the snow and ice off of my driver's side window before I could unlock it and start it up. While the car warmed up, with the defroster on high, I brushed the snow off of the entire car and scraped the windows as clean as I could get them. I went back into the apartment foyer and grabbed my laptop bag and the notebook. A few minutes later I was pulling into the store parking lot. The roads were better than expected, the parking lot- worse. I struggled on the slippery spots to keep my footing, trying to keep my balance with my hands full. A kind elderly gentleman who was exiting the store held the door for me. Once inside, I shook off the cold and headed to my right, and straight into the Starbucks for a cup of steaming heaven on earth.

I stood at the counter and placed my usual order. I always opted for either a French vanilla cappuccino or latte... today I chose the cappuccino. It may have been a subconscious suggestion from my sleepy headed son. Whatever the case, I chose it without thinking. While the barista finished making my drink, I turned to find an open table. I was pleasantly surprised to be waved over by all three of my teammates who had already secured a booth in the corner, away from almost everyone else. I walked over to the table and emptied my hands, just as they called out that my drink was ready. I took the cup in both hands and felt its warmth penetrate into my still icy fingers. I took the open seat at the booth next to Theo.

"I'm sure you are all wondering why I gathered you here today." I spouted a line I had used at seminars in the past but today I only received blank looks from my friends. "That was supposed to be funny."

"Why *did* you get us all out in this nasty weather?" Jenn asked, half serious, half sarcastically.

"Well, this is going to sound weird..." I began.

"Uh... we're all weird, so go head." Katie teased.

"Okay... the other night, I had this freaky dream, and you were all in it, but like ghosts." I waited for the raised eye brow looks. Instead I saw looks of surprise on everyone's faces.

"Uh, me too." Theo said curiously.

"Really. So did I, and Ash was there with a little boy." Jenn added.

"Right?" Katie put her hand on her forehead. "What the heck is going on here? I mean, we all had the same dream kinda."

"Let me get Hilary on Skype, and we'll talk to her about it, but what I got from the dream was that we had to get back to the Infirmary ASAP." I fired up the laptop and connected to the store's free wi-fi. Once connected, I double-clicked the Skype icon, logged in and placed the video call to Hilary.

"Well, it's about damn time!" She laughed through her smart-assed opening line.

"Well, hello to you too." I snapped back at her, pushing the laptop to the far end of the booth, against the wall. "We all made it."

"How's the weather up there?" Theo leaned over in front of the screen to speak to Hilary. When he said the words 'up there' it dawned on me why Hilary said what she opened up the conversation with. We were in different time zones, and noon here was 1 pm there, so we had kept her waiting for an hour.

"Sorry Hil... I forgot about the time change. I told you noon, but it's noon here, not there." I quickly apologized.

"That's alright Rick... and Theo, it's northern Ohio... so it's freakin' cold as hell." She said in her usual tone, not realizing the irony of her statement. "So, tell me what's going on... Why the special meeting?"

144

"Hey Hilary, it's Jenn." She leaned in and waved to the screen. "It seems we all had the same dream Friday night."

"Well, that's just creepy." She responded. "I don't remember dreaming anything the past few nights."

"And, in the dream our friend, Ashley told us we needed to hurry up and get back to the Infirmary to help the spirits there." Katie added leaning onto her elbow.

"Okay. You guys are welcome to come up anytime, but it's about zero freakin' degrees here, for a high." Hilary was being cordial and brutally honest at the same time. "...and who's your friend Ashley?"

"Ashley is a little girl, a ghost, we helped a while back, and now she tries to help us sometimes." Theo explained. "There was a real urgency in what she said, and she was holding the hand of a little boy. Any idea who that might be?"

"Not really. There weren't any records of kids dying here, but I guess there might have been." Hilary thought for a minute, but got sidetracked. "Hey! I have a new piece for you to check out, I haven't showed anybody yet, not even Mike. If you're coming up soon, I'll just show you then."

"Alright, I'm guessing it's something really good, huh?" I finally managed to get the words out.

"Oh yeah. It's creepy as hell, and it's about Maddie." She smiled, knowing how much I wanted her to just tell me what it was.

"Okay... so, when can everyone find time to take a day and a half, or two to go to the Infirmary?" I posed the question to everyone.

"I can make time whenever." Theo answered first.

"Um, not next weekend, but maybe the one after that." Katie gave her answer.

"I could do that weekend, but I have a Delegate meeting in

Indianapolis the weekend after that, so...yeah." I left it at that and waited to hear what Jenn had to say.

"I make the schedules out at work, and this is our slow time, so I can take that weekend off, no problem." Jenn said happily.

I leaned in to look directly at Hilary. "How about two weeks from yesterday? That'd be...." I looked at the calendar on my phone. "...April 3rd."

"Sure. I'm always off on Sundays, and if I work on Saturday, we close at 4, so I'd be home by 5 at the latest." Hilary confirmed our plan.

"Alright then... we have a road trip to plan!" Jenn interjected.

"Woot Woot!" Katie cheered pumping her fists into the air in celebration.

"Okay... Guess I'll see you in a couple weeks. See you all later." Hilary waved good-bye as she ended the video call.

"Well, we have a date." I was thrilled.

"Again..." Said Jenn, remembering how poorly our last planned road trip worked out.

"Well, I'm going to have to be at death's door to miss this trip." Katie joked. "And, if the boys are sick, they can just go stay with Nana."

"So, what your saying is, if you aren't on death's door step, you are coming with us to death's door step... and right on in to death's house." Theo was being sarcastic, not his usual trait, but we all picked up on how true his statement was.

"We all know how hard it is to get an investigation planned this far out of town. We need to figure out what we are going to do to try to bring these souls peace while we are there." I tossed the thought out and waited for the feedback.

"Sage, sweet grass and cedar smudging, for sure." Jenn said, and I nodded, winked and pointed at her.

"Holy water and white candle blessings." Katie added.

"Great ideas." I agreed with them all. "We should probably bring sea salts and some lavender too."

"I can prepare some blessing prayers and rituals, and of course we could connect with the spirits and encourage them to crossover into the light." Theo knew how important verbally explaining the process and saying the right ritualistic prayers out loud could be, being the team psychic and ordained minister.

"Again, great ideas. I have one other suggestion... Ashley." I looked around the table, but no one wanted to respond or even make eye contact with me. "I mean, she helped us before, and she came to all of us in our dreams this time... maybe she is supposed to help."

"You're probably right, it's just a little frightening to think of the powers at the infirmary and her powers in the same place..." Theo's words trailed off with his thoughts.

"No doubt." Katie agreed. "That little girl scares the hell outta me!"

"Well then, if she could just scare the *hell* out of that place, maybe we'd have a better chance." Theo once again jested and was serious at the same time.

"What about trying to find out where Maddie is buried and mark her grave somehow... say a blessing over her remains?" Jenn thought out loud.

"So many unmarked graves, and we don't even know where some of them are. That may be impossible, but it's definitely worth giving it every effort." I thought she had a brilliant idea.

"I have one other suggestion. I'm going to send you all a calendar spreadsheet. Try to fill in everything you remember about the investigation, newspaper clippings, dreams, conversations... whatever is relevant, under the date that it belongs, or as close as you can guess. Then email them back to me a few days before we go to Ohio, like Thursday. I'll merge the data together. I'll send it to Hilary and have her and Mike do the same thing. Maybe if we go over the whole time line before we head to the Infirmary, it might help." I had homework for everyone, but no one seemed to mind.

"You know we are all going to have a lot of the same stuff, so when you merge them, it's going to be pretty repetitive." Jenn pointed out.

"That's true, but that's why I want it by Thursday. I can go through it Friday night and hopefully delete all of the identical info. If that isn't enough, I would really like for you all to put in your personal opinions about things, and..." I looked to Theo. "...any psychic impressions would be greatly appreciated."

Everyone agreed and soon we were headed our separate ways. We had been at Barnes & Noble just long enough that my car was completely cold again. I turned the key, and the cold air blasted out of the defroster, which I had accidentally left on high. "Holy crap!" I shouted out to myself as I shivered and quickly switched the fan to its lowest setting. I pulled out of the parking lot and made a bee-line for the nearest gas station where I could get my son a French vanilla cappuccino. He preferred the gas station version over the pricey coffee shop cappuccinos. I completely understood. From a young person's point of view, the gas station ones were much sweeter and had more vanilla flavor. I left the car running while I ran in to get his drink. I was pleasantly surprised to return to find my car warming up nicely.

When I walked in the front door, Daniel dropped his game remote in the middle of playing and reached out with both hands, licking his lips.

"I didn't think you'd ever get home." He took the cup from my hand before I could even get my keys back in my pocket.

"I was only gone an hour, and you were sleeping when I left." I smiled at him. He was growing up so fast, but somewhere inside, he was still my little boy.

"Nu uh.. you woke me up before you left." He corrected me.

"Yeah, but I thought you went back to sleep." I said honestly.

"I did try, but I kept thinking about you bringing me a cappuccino, and I just couldn't fall back asleep, so I've been gaming and waiting for you to get home." He finally stopped sipping at the hot drink and picked his game controller up again, and was soon lost in his cyber-world, shooting Nazi zombies.

I retreated to my room and quickly created the spread sheet. Once I had emailed it out to everyone, I sent Hilary a text explaining what I needed. She quickly responded with a 'sure thing'. When I had that behind me, I sat down to start filling out my own time line. I worked on it in between doing the weekend chores and cooking dinner. I was nearly finished by the end of the night, and knew I could wrap it up in the next evening or two. The upcoming trip already had me excited and nervous, and honestly a bit terrified. I knew the next two weeks would drag by, but it would not be nearly as long as it had been.

Photo by Rick Kueber

CHAPTER 11

AS WE SEE IT

Over the next two weeks I had been able to make arrangements for my son for the weekend and managed to prepare for the road trip to Ohio. I had merged and edited all of the data from everyone's spread sheets and printed out enough copies for everyone. I had not read every word of the time line, but had a good idea of its contents. I was surprised by some of the input that I was unaware of, and impressed by the overall story it told.

When Friday evening came, I took my son over to stay with his friend for the weekend, returned home and packed up my things for my weekend trip. By process of elimination, we had decided to take Theo's car back to Ohio. Jenn traded her Camry for a newer convertible and it would have been a tight squeeze, Katie's truck would only fit three people, and I wasn't sure if my car would make it without a breakdown. My apartment had been chosen as a meeting point. It had plenty of open parking and lots of neighbors to keep an eye on the cars while we were away. As it worked out, Theo arrived first around 9 am, much to my astonishment. While I loaded my cases into his trunk, Katie zipped in next to Theo's Subaru. She popped out of her truck and hastily grabbed her things out of the passenger side of the truck cab.

"Hang on! I'll be right there." She yelled over to us.

"No biggie." I laughed. "Jenn isn't even here yet."

"Surprise, surprise." Theo grinned.

Still in a rush, she tossed her case into the trunk and a shoulder bag into the back seat. Katie let out an audible sigh as if she had been stressed about being on time and was now relieved that all she had to do was climb in the car and relax for the long drive. She looked up to the clear sky as she walked over and locked up her truck.

"Who would have thought it would be this nice out? I think winter is finally ending." She said returning to where we were congregated in the parking lot.

"I know. Maybe we won't actually freeze to death tonight." Theo half joked, thinking about our first trip to the Infirmary.

The sound of a passing car on the street in front of the apartment complex with its stereo cranked up and blasting 80's hair-rock music caught our attention. The music grew louder as Jenn pulled around the corner in her new silver convertible. The top was up, but the music was still quite loud. She whipped around us and took the nearest open spot she could find. Jenn waved as she stepped out of the car, sliding her sunglasses from their proper place to the top of her head.

"Hey kids!" She called out. Her tone was as perky and cheery as I had heard it in a very long time. "Who's ready for this?"

"ME!" Katie shouted back to her while Theo and I meekly raised our hands in acknowledgment.

"Right on time as always." I teased.

152

"Shut up, E-V-Prick... I'm not that late." She rolled her eyes sarcastically as she passed by with bags in hand, bumping hard into me with her hard sided equipment case, knocking me off balance enough to stumble back a step or two. When she had her case securely placed in the trunk, Theo closed it and with a push of a button, unlocked the car doors and everyone began to open them, selecting their places. I was taking shotgun.

"Oh hell!" I jumped back out of the car. "I almost forgot to lock the apartment." I took a few steps and turned back. "Anyone need to use the restroom before we head out."

"Oh, me!" Katie popped out, followed by Jenn who chimed in. "Me too."

"The slider's open." I looked down to Theo, still in the driver's seat, and shrugged my shoulders.

When the girls finally emerged together, I went in and locked up the apartment. Being all loaded up and buckled in, we headed out on an adventure we could not even imagine being truly prepared for. The first interstate we headed out on, I-64, was the same one that led us to the Helmach house in West Virginia. There was an overwhelming and mutual feeling between us. The last time we were all headed down this highway, we were on our way to our most terrifying investigation ever.

The radio was playing quietly in the background, and was nearly drowned out by the hum of the highway. Very few words were spoken during the first three hours of the trip. When we exited onto I-71 the mood changed drastically. Even the air felt lighter. One stop for lunch and two rest-stop breaks later and we were pulling into the small town of Bangs, Ohio. It was still a gorgeous day, though it was nearing sunset by the time we were turning into the long driveway at Mike and Hilary's home.

"Well hell." I thought out loud, pulling my phone out of my pocket. "I was supposed to call her when we left and text when we got close."

Jenn stuck her arm up between Theo and I, pointing to the house.

"Well, we're close." Her sarcasm had us all smiling, so I sent a text anyway.

"We're close." -Rick

"How close?" -Hil

"About 100 ft from your door." -Rick

Without another text, the front door flew open and Hilary rushed out. It had been a couple of years since the girls met Hilary and Mike. The reunion was emotional, exciting and carried all the way into the front room. When all of the 'good to see you's and 'welcome back's were through, we settled into the comfort of their overstuffed couches and the array of chairs they had assembled. Our talks bounced back and forth with no particular direction. The only constant was that after the first few minutes, it was focused entirely on the haunting of the Infirmary, Maddie, and even little Ash, the burning girl. I had only brought in a file folder with me, but I opened it and began to pass out the stapled pages of the spreadsheets.

"Well, this is going to be pretty interesting, exciting and even enlightening to probably everybody." I began what would turn into a very long monologue, telling the story, as we knew it. "Unless you already know everything here." I looked over to Theo with a smile.

"I'm sure it will be an education for us all." He smiled back as he thumbed through the black and white printed pages.

"I think you can follow along with me if you want, but I'm going to kind of 'ad-lib' so it flows together a little better." And so, I began to tell the story that had even Hilary herself wide eyed and on the edge of her seat. The tale began with a dream that Theo had sent me as part of his time-line, a dream that took place in the very room where we now sat to learn the story as we knew it.

***

The civil war was nearing its end when a confederate troop made camp in the foothills of the Appalachian mountains. As the war efforts began to slow and the killing of brothers lessened, the negative, evil energies of war began to concentrate where it could. In this camp in particular, the evil became a beast, and that beast drained the life from every single soldier, save one. The evil energy had become an entity and that entity had intelligence. The man was left alive with intentions. The beast pursued him through the forest, but it knew there would be a chance that the elements would claim this man's life as well. The beast, conscious of the mortality of its newly found intelligence, split its energy in half. One half fled the wilds of the forest as swift as lightning and was drawn to the closest energy of the living... Summersville, West Virginia. This half of the entity again divided itself into several, slightly weaker, energies and attached themselves to average everyday people, not taking them over or causing irreparable damage...yet. The beast planned to let these individuals fall on hard times of one sort or another and seek help from the church. One by one they would infiltrate, and begin to bend and twist the minds of the congregation, eventually leading to a witch hunt that could destroy more lives and more faith from within, and to the beast, that was wickedly satisfying. It studied the townsfolk from within themselves and found two young girls with unique powers of their own, and it made a plan to control the energies and powers of these young souls. It would stop at nothing to have them.

The other half followed and soon caught the soldier. Its evil powers drove the man night and day until he had made it to a small settlement on the edge of the Ohio River, where he found refuge. Over the next several years, the man fell on a string of hard times, and bad luck. He went from town to town, begging for food and shelter until the constable or other authority would run him out of town. His final destination was Bangs, Ohio. There was a poor house and farm that took him in and he lived there, keeping to himself quietly, until his odd and nervous behaviors were noticed by the Infirmary psychiatrist who had him committed as an inmate. This half of the beast soon dispersed itself amongst the many insane inmates and even some of the staff. In the minds of the staff it would cause them to commit cruel and evil acts that went unnoticed or disbelieved by those who heard the tales from the inmates, assuming the stories were made up or caused by their mental disorders. This gave the beast a twisted pleasure that it craved like an addiction.

~

It was summertime in the mid 1870's, when a young girl named Ashley Sue Helmach made a new friend. She had been in town while her father was at the general store to pick up the monthly dry goods. She stood outside, as her father had asked, when she noticed a girl sitting alone at the corner of the store. She approached the young girl who was a few years older than she was and could sense her unhappiness. The girl was afraid of being judged and outcast, or worse, because she had the ability at times to see the spirits of those who had died as clearly as she could see the living. This had caused confusion and trouble in the past when her parents, teachers, and even her pastor had asked who she was speaking to or about. At her young age, she did not know that others didn't see them.

Ashley knew exactly how it felt to be different and unaccepted by others. To comfort her, she offered the girl her mother's blessed, moonstone and silver necklace to comfort and protect her. Ashley introduced herself to the girl, and the young girl replied, saying her name was Taylor Madison. Perhaps this has nothing to do with the story of Madison Taylor, or perhaps it is everything.

~

The years passed until one wintery day a young woman around twenty years of age arrived, half dead, on the doorstep of the Infirmary in the early morning hours, well before dawn. She held a little boy in her arms and called out for help. So weak from not having eaten and having traveled so far, exposed to the elements, she placed the boy on the doorstep and pounded her fists against the door, screaming for help until her voice was in shreds and her hands began to leave bloody prints on the pristine white front doors of the Infirmary.

The night watchman peered out the window, hoping no one else would hear the pounding and cries of the woman. Her strength eventually gave out and she lost consciousness. When she had been motionless for nearly an hour, the watchman opened the door and scrubbed the bloody marks from it. After closing and locking the door again, he called out for the orderly on duty. The two men carried the limp body of the woman inside and placed her on a cot. The orderly checked her for a pulse and finding her to be alive, covered her with a gray woolen blanket. The watchman stayed with her while the orderly returned to where the boy laid still on the front step. He knelt down beside the boy and felt the cold, puddled rain soaking through the knees of his white uniform pants. The man's breath was a steamy white and as he knelt there, shivering, he noticed no winter breath coming from the child.

The dawn was breaking over the horizon, casting a dull glow on the damp world below. The attending psychiatrist had awakened a short time earlier and still in his robe, wandered down the stairs. He had made it a habit of visiting the industrial kitchen to acquire a hot cup of freshly brewed coffee before preparing himself for his day. When he reached the main floor, near the entrance he encountered the watchman and was informed of the orderly's whereabouts. Still barefoot, he ran to the front door and found the orderly leaning over the boy.

"Dead." The orderly said, showing no emotion.

"And the woman inside, what of her?" The Dr. asked with a grim look.

"She was alive when we carried her in, but she didn't look well." He said coldly.

"Call the caretaker. Get the boy buried before anyone sees. I will talk with the night watch and we will tell no one of the boy. If the woman survives the day, we will tell her there **was** no boy. Perhaps she will not remember how or when she arrived here. I think it would be better for her to not know, than to think this child was dead." The psychiatrist assumed to know what was best, or perhaps there was a deeper evil driving his decision, unbeknownst

157

to him.

Maddie's time as an inmate at the Infirmary passed painfully slow. The ghosts of the Infirmary were distraught, and called out for her help, and with each passing month, their numbers grew, as other inmates passed away. There were two spirits that troubled her the most... two spirits that she never saw, but was always looking over her shoulder for and nervously darting looks out of the corners of her eyes at every movement. One spirit she hoped she would see, and the other, she prayed she would never face. These unsettling visions and absences, combined with the lies she had been filled with about the fate of the child she arrived with, gave the doctors the predisposition to commit her permanently for a disorder that was labeled in the 1800's as 'Nervousness'. Something that would have been treated with simple medications in modern times, and would have allowed a normal and productive life... something Maddie had been denied since childhood.

Late one night, when the Infirmary had gone nearly silent, Maddie was locked in her room, still awake. The full moon was high and bright, and there was a stellar energy in the air. Another energy was in the air that night...yet not so heavenly. The evil force that shadowed the residents and caretakers at the Infirmary was growing stronger this night. The entity that had split itself into so many different bits of negative energy had slipped from its 'home' in the attending psychiatrist, and was once again assembling its shattered energies to maximize its power and carry out a most heinous act. When the beast was once again whole, it slipped past the few awake attendees and night guard and directly into the room of a former civil war soldier named Adam. When the beast had taken over Adam's body, he was able to do simple tasks that were impossible from the spiritual plane. As Adam unobtrusively passed the dozing guard, the beast grew confident of its plan. It would soon take the life of the second gifted little girl, and it was certain it would then have her soul. A patient of the infirmary, who was not committed, spotted Adam in the hallway. The elderly man stepped out to call for the guard, or an orderly, knowing the inmates weren't allowed to roam the halls so late at night, and never unattended. Using Adam's flesh as his own, the beast wrapped Adam's fingers around the man's throat and found it so effortless to squeeze the life out of him. The beast smiled through Adam's face, his eyes glazed in a sinister and insane stare, while he watched the old man's face turn beet red, while his struggle diminished. He glared into the man's eyes as they lost their color, becoming gray and hazed over.

The beast was not able to steal the man's soul, it was free and passed into a light that was so brilliant, the beast could not bear to be in its presence. The evil entity retreated in rage and a tinge of fear. Its pace quickened as the beast brutally murdered two more innocent people in its quest for Madison. When Adam, and the beast within, were trapped in the room next to Maddie's, the beast grew frustrated. The popping sound of the night guard's pistol surprised the beast with a new sensation. There was a burning feeling in the borrowed flesh of Adam. The beast cast the physical body of Adam aside, discarding it out of the fourth story window without a second thought, like a stale and unwanted crust of bread thrown to the trash.

Madison cowered in the corner of her room and watched the beast pass straight through the wall, something it could not do in the confines of Adams physical body. The blackness of the beast towered over her, instilling its fear into her heart. She trembled with fright, shooting glances all about the room, looking for another soul, who she assumed was controlling this devil. Silently, the tears streamed down her face as she prepared to have herself shredded into ribbons of red lifeless flesh. There was no desire for death in her heart, and a fear of the hell that awaited her in the afterlife consumed her thoughts. In spite of those fears, Maddie opened up. She leaned back, spread her arms wide and waited for the beast to deliver its stinging and tormenting death. When her arms opened as wide as she could spread them, she arched her back, protruding her chest. The tie at the neckline of her drab gown came undone and the silver and moonstone necklace was exposed. Infuriated and confounded the entity cowered away from the brightly glowing pendant. Some form of powerful magic, that the beast was unfamiliar with, protected the woman-child, and a feeling it had never known had it befuddled... until this moment it had never truly known fear. The dark and evil beast retreated into the shadows, dispersed itself into the living tenants and patiently waited for opportunity to call it back into being.

While the time passed, the beast found ways to pacify itself by possessing other inmates and causing them to take their own lives. It reveled in the feel of the cold and broken shard of glass in the hand of a man locked in his apartment on the fourth floor one night. It made the man press the razor sharp and burred edge against his neck, slowly slicing and ripping at his own throat until he bled out. His soul, very aware of the powers of this demon, remained at the Infirmary under the control of the beast, like so many others before him had done.

On a fateful night in January, when two orderlies were put on the task of the hot and cold bath therapy for Madison, the beast knew his opportunity had arisen. The evil entity gathered itself together into one, as it had done before.

"Come on princess... time to get you stripped down, scrubbed up and down in the therapy baths, then off to bed for you." Harold said in a cruel tone.

"Princess? She ain't no princess, my friend. This here's Queen Madison, but I think 'Maddie' is more appropriate." Spouted the second orderly, Edgar,

"Oh my! Well, beggin' your pardon madam. I didn't realize you were royalty!" Harold said as he let go a boisterous laugh.

"Yes... forgive him, your Royal Madness!" Edgar taunted as they pulled her from the floor, unwillingly.

It followed the men as they dragged Maddie reluctantly into the therapy room. Inside the room, with the door closed and locked, the beast divided its energy between the men, and having the convenience of flesh and bone, it was able to forcefully torture and abuse the young woman until she had nearly no fight or life left in her. She had been stripped of her gown and was completely naked and exposed. The protecting necklace hung limp from her neck, mimicking her lifeless body on the table. Using the flesh of one of the men, the beast was able to rip the necklace from her, dropping it to the floor, where it would remain while they dressed the battered and mistreated woman. The two men escorted her back to her room, soaking wet, bruised and ashamed. They locked her in her apartment, but not before taking her blankets and pillow, out of inhumane cruelty.

Moments after the men had left Maddie's room, the beast left them. Realizing what he had done, Harold rushed to the therapy room, snatched up the necklace and returned to Maddie's room. He entered the room, and the small framed young woman crouched away from him, whimpering when he came close. The chain was broken, but ruefulness and embarrassment over took the man, and he gingerly laid the necklace against her still damp flesh, and retreated, backing out of the room sheepishly. Upon entering the corridor, he locked Maddie's door and with his face turned to the floor, quickly left the fourth floor ward.

The evil beast was enraged by the cowardly weakness of human emotion and regret. Once again his plans to take the life and soul of this woman-child had been undone. Though the power of the necklace kept him from entering her, there was another way. The beast used the negative power of its energy like an unimaginably powerful electromagnet, causing the tubes within the radiant heater to collapse in on themselves, blocking the flow of steam. The beast filled the corner of the room and grew larger and stronger while the room grew more frigid by the minute. Soon, Madison's breath poured from her like smoke from raging inferno, and frost began to cover the inside of the windows. She tried to warm herself by pulling herself tightly into a fetal position. Sinister laughter filled the air as Madison's heart slowed and the moisture from her 'therapy' began to form icy crystals in her hair first, then her eyelashes, and then on her frostbitten and frozen fingers and toes. Hours were spent in excruciating pain while she felt herself slowly freezing to death.

The beast let out an audible screech of triumph when it collected Maddie's soul. It remained in the room, reveling in victory

161

over her frost covered body, before taking her spirit to the lowest level of the Infirmary where it had collected the lost souls together to reign over them. In this dank and dreary place where the old boilers were located and the mice gathered together to take shelter from the harsh Ohio winter, it instilled in them, once again, its power over them, and easily swayed them to believe this was their eternal home. Most of the souls it had taken were discarded paupers, and it was all too simple for them to be persuaded that they were outcasts, loved by no one, claimed by no friends or family in death, and so detested their bodies had been buried carelessly into unmarked graves in unnoticed cemeteries.

Maddie believed that this eternal hell was her penance for the wrongs she had done in her life, and did not fight for her peace. She did quickly scan the room of lost souls for the boy, and she found solace in his absence.

Harold heard the cry of the beast as it took Maddie's life and soul. With a fear of being called out for his part in her abuse, he shot down the iron stairwell. His shoes made a loud echoing racket as he clambered down floor by floor, searching the corridors until he found Edgar, his partner in the night's evils deeds.

"Somethin's goin' on in Madison's room. If she gets too loud, somebody's gonna find her in there...she might tell 'em what happened." He nervously spoke in a hushed tone.

"Right..." Edgar said, looking side to side, checking the ward for activity. "Let's go."

The men climbed the spinning staircase swiftly and took care to not be noticed. Reaching the fourth floor, Edgar watched for the night guard while Harold fumbled through his large ring of countless brass keys. When he located the correct key, the two men crept over to her door. The key was silently slid into the lock and with a quick jingle and a metallic snap, the lock gave in to the desires of the orderlies. With ease and care, the door opened slightly. Frosty air escaped through the opening, and an overpowering sense of fear and death overtook the two.

"Princess... are you awake?" Harold whispered.

"Can you hear us? May we come in, your Royal Maddness?" Edgar asked politely, not realizing he had called her by the cruel name used so many times in the past.

A sub-zero chill and silence was the only reply. Nervously looking over their shoulder again, the men slipped into the room, closing and locking the door behind them. Striking a match to light an oil lamp on the wall, the air filled with the smell of sulfur. The men rubbed their hands together to warm their already numbing fingers. They found Maddie's frost covered form, curled up in a fetal position and frozen to her bed sheet. Approaching the piece of furniture, they began to realize their worst fears.

"It's awfully cold in here princess... you alright?" Harold said to her, placing his hand on the curve of her shoulder. He felt the blood drain from his face and a deeply sickening feeling turned his stomach.

"She okay?" Asked Edgar.

"Dead...she's frozen stiff." He choked out, while his mind raced with the current and future consequences of their actions.

"We can't take the blame for this... What are we gonna do?" Edgar asked.

"It's over... we deserve what we get." Harold whimpered.

"NO!" Edgar almost shouted. "Help me... I got an idea."

Edgar grabbed at Madison and began to peel her away from the bed sheet. Unwillingly, Harold began to help, but the moisture had frozen the sheet to her icy blue flesh and bits of skin and chunks of flesh tore away from her, frozen to the sheet, like fileting the flesh away from the skin of a catfish. She had been so drenched and frozen so solidly to the sheet, Edgar snapped both of her arms trying to release it from her grasp. When their effort had finally freed the sheet from her frozen and now mangled body, Edgar opened the window.

"Give me a hand Harold." He motioned Harold to grab the lower half of Madison while he pulled her upper body and head away from the mattress like ripping a piece of Velcro from its counter piece. Even without the presence of the beast, Edgar was such a twisted individual, he nearly laughed when he lifted her from the bed.

"Looky here, Harold. Her hair is frozen stiff just like she's still laying on the bed." He pointed out the morose feature, which only weakened Harold's knees.

The two men had no trouble carrying the tiny woman to the opened window where her glaciated corpse was tossed out. Her head hit first, snapping her neck completely backwards, and the rest of her body crushed into the icy snow with the sound of several popping bones.

"You think they'll believe she killed herself?" Harold questioned Edgar's plan.

Edgar unlocked the wardrobe and pulled out a hat and scarf. He studied the situation before carefully dropping them out the window and watching them land in the snow just feet away from Maddie.

"There." He said smugly. "She tried to run away twice before. Now they'll just think she was escaping again." He left the window open. "Now let's get outta here before somebody sees we're missing."

The two orderlies looked over the room carefully, and wrapped the flesh dotted sheet as tightly as they could. Being as silent as possible in the predawn hours, they cracked the door open ever so slightly to spy into the hallway for unwanted onlookers. The world of the Infirmary was asleep, and the two sneaked down into the subterranean level of the building.

"Damn it Harold, it's cold as heck down here." Edgar expressed his surprise.

"Somethings off. You think the boiler needs coal, or is broke down? It feels spooky down here... Maybe everybody's froze to death." Harold replied, as his face began to pale again.

"You are the biggest sissy I know, Harold." Edgar shot back at him. "We ain't dead are we? The halls weren't cold were they? It's probably just the Mad girl's room. Now, fire up that incinerator and let's get rid of this evidence."

"Right." Harold splashed a bit of kerosene on the sheet and tossed it and a few bits of a broken chair into the incinerator. Striking a large wooden match, the sheet and wooden pieces were consumed in the fiery pit. Returning upstairs, Harold placed a new sheet on Maddie's bed, and returned her pillow and blanket. He was confused to find the room was once again warming, though the frost of winter still crept in through the opened window.

The local authorities, with the assistance of head officiant of the Infirmary, concurred with the story of the night shift orderlies, and the newspaper story confirmed the falsified facts.

A shallow hole was arduously dug in the hard, January earth, and her remains were hidden in one of the countless unmarked graves. As fate would have it, she did not remain there long. Two days had passed when two young gentlemen arrived in a horse drawn wagon to exhume her cadaver. The beast and Madison's spirit looked on while her corpse was loaded onto the wagon and began to pull away. Madison stepped up, spooking the horse for a moment, when the evil entity whispered a terrible thought into her consciousness...

"You do not belong... you have been lost your entire life... unwanted... an outcast."

Suddenly, so many thoughts flooded back to her. Her family had been outcasts in their home town and were forced to leave. When she feared it would happen again, she betrayed her only friend, but that only made her fears worsen. To save her family the heartache of being run out of another town, she took it upon herself to run away... but her family did not come looking for her, even though she had stayed in the woods near their home for several days. Then something terrified her, and she ran farther and farther away. She wandered for a very long time, searching for a place to fit in. When she thought she had found a friend, that did not end well either, as the boy died in her arms on the steps of the infirmary. Everyone she had ever loved either died or had forgotten about her... except for the beast. Every place she had tried to call home, she had been forced to move on from...except the Infirmary... and now, her body was being taken from it.

The horses pulled the wagon onto the main road and when they began to trot at a quicker pace, Maddie's spirit flew in front of the two horse team screaming. "Nooooo!"

The horses spooked causing the wagon to overturn and one of the men to be dragged down the road. The other man was overtaken by the beast and scrambled to hide Madison's body in the ditch, covering her in a thick layer of snow.

"Don't leave me here!" Madison's specter called out to the Infirmary attendants who were returning to the warmth of the building, not even noticing the incident.

"Lost again..." The beast whispered to her. "You belong here with the other souls... you belong to me." She stayed with her corpse in the ditch waiting to be found, but when the days passed, and no one came, she returned to the confines of the infirmary... she returned to the beast... and there is where she remains to this day...

"And I think that brings us up to date with everything we know, everything we think we know, and a few things I am assuming to know." I sat back, drew a deep breath and met the eyes of everyone, one at a time.

CHAPTER 12
HIDDEN GEMS

My eyes caught Hilary's last. A blank look was on her face, and her eyes were wide with pupils dilated and black. She opened her mouth to speak but nothing came out. We all looked at each other, shrugging shoulders and raising eyebrows when Hilary stood up silently and disappeared into the other room.

"Where's she going?" I directed my question to Mike.

"Hell if I know." He stated bluntly, looking over his shoulder to the doorway she had exited through.

Hilary quickly returned to the living room with a notebook and file folder in her hand. She quietly took her seat again and began to fumble through the files and documents. She stopped suddenly and fondled the page in her hand nervously.

"How did you know?" Four simple words was all she said as she handed me the photo copy of the newspaper article.

EXCITING RUNAWAY

Serious Mishap to Medical Students Who

Were After Material For Dissecting Purposes

"This was the 'new discovery' I was telling you about. It tells all about the wagon accident when two med students came to get Maddie's body to dissect for studies at the local Medical College. It is almost exactly like the story you told... even about them losing her body in the ditch and not returning to get it." Hilary explained. "So... how the hell did you know?"

I didn't say a word, but looked over at Mike.

"That was me..." He began.

"You shit!" Hilary smacked the back of his head with her open hand. "I was going to surprise them with this new evidence. You've been going through my stuff?"

"No, I swear." Mike said honestly, but with a smile at her frustration. "I sent it to him with the time line he asked for... it was a dream I had... remember when we all went to the Infirmary, and the next morning I told you I had a crazy dream, but then couldn't remember it?"

"Ummm... yeah... but you couldn't remember it, right?" Hilary spouted off sarcastically.

"Nice... good come back." Jenn smiled, appreciating good sarcasm.

"Well, when I was trying to think of anything I knew about the Infirmary, it just came to me...every detail." He justified the reason to her and it was well accepted that he was being 100% truthful.

"Well, I have a couple of other things to tell you." Hilary continued, directing her dialogue to me. "There is a reality ghost T.V. show that wants to do an episode at the Infirmary, and they want you and me to

168

join them."

"Wow... that's cool." I said deep in thought and memory. Could this have been what Ash was meaning when she talked about someone exploiting the spirits? "Will have to see how it works out, but sounds interesting."

"The other thing was the boy... there was a psychic here a few years ago, and she claimed that Maddie was haunted by a little boy and took her own life, but I didn't put much faith in what she said. Maybe she was right about the boy, but I had documents that went against just about everything else she claimed about the Infirmary residents, but that story you compiled... I think you nailed it." Hilary showed her trust in me and my team.

"No." I disagreed. "We nailed it. There was only a small part of that story that was mine... it's not my story."

"You put it together, though." Mike added.

"But we all told it." Katie clarified.

"You're right Rick... and Katie... and Mike." Jenn began, and I expected a smart-ass remark. "We all told it, you put it together nicely, but it's not your story, it never was... It was always Maddie's story."

"Right." Theo agreed. "And, as great of a story as it is... I just want to point out that it's been dark for a while and we have a lot of work to do tonight."

"Yeah, and a long drive home tomorrow, so we'd better get this party started." Katie had a way of lightening the most solemn situations.

"I'm ready if everybody else is..." Hilary posed the statement like a question to us all, but turned to Mike as she said it.

"I'm ready." Mike said. "Anybody want a bottle of water for the road?"

Most of us nodded, but Hilary said, "Just throw a bunch in a cooler and let's go."

Mike handed her the keys to the truck and headed to the kitchen to grab the waters out of the fridge. The rest of us followed Hilary out to the garage. With a push of a button, the automatic garage door opener engaged, making a loud mechanical hum.

"We can all squeeze in the truck if you want." Hilary called out as she unlocked the truck doors.

"We could... but it would be easier and probably more comfortable to drive separately." Theo said. "We do have a lot of junk in the trunk."

"Oh my god!" Jenn burst out.

"That was hilarious!" Katie said while I tried to contain my laughter.

"Well..."Theo shrugged his shoulders with a grin so huge, his eyes squinted. "... It's true." At that point, everyone burst out laughing, as Mike walked out of the door, into the garage.

"What's so funny?" He asked with an odd look.

"You had to be there." I said when my laughter subsided. "Okay, we'll follow you... which way?"

Mike pointed toward the end of the driveway, and then motioned to the left. We all loaded into the car and truck and backed out of the long and narrow driveway. Theo backed out and to the right far enough to let Mike get the truck out with plenty of extra room, and with the 'pop' of switching gears, we were on our way to a date with destiny... maybe not ours, but someone's destiny. It seemed like a longer drive this time than it did on our first visit, but it was still a very short trip compared to our long road trip to Hilary and Mike's home. Mike and Hilary made the last turn of our journey with our car-full right behind them.

"Almost there." Theo's voice was filled with emotion.

"Where?" Jenn and Katie yelled out from the back seat and the heads of both girls popped up in between Theo and I, straining to see through the windshield.

"I don't see it." Katie said disappointingly.

"There." I pointed to the pinpoint of the dusk to dawn light. Their eyes squinted through the darkness to catch a glimpse of history. They glared silently through the windshield as we bumped down the road. The trees were barren, but the hill behind the Infirmary and the direction of the parking lot light kept it hidden in the darkness until we turned in to park.

"Holy crap!" Jenn blurted out upon seeing the massive structure.

"Oh.... wow..." Katie said out loud, to herself. "It's kinda overwhelming in person."

"Just wait... overwhelming is an understatement." I said slyly as I opened the door, letting the cold come crashing in.

We all piled out of the car, and Theo popped the trunk open. Mike and Hilary reluctantly left the warmth of their truck with flashlights in hand, and joined us at the back of the silver-blue Subaru. We had decided to only take cameras, candles, sage and holy water with us. Tonight, we were on a mission, not an investigation.

"Damn it's cold!" Jenn stated the obvious.

"Ha!" Hilary laughed. "This isn't bad."

"Yeah, you should have been here last time... and it was even colder inside than it was outside." What Theo said was very true. It was noticeably warmer. Hilary and I shot a look at each other. The memory of nearly freezing to death came rushing back.

"You all ready for this shit?" Mike yelled out, making us cringe away slightly.

Ready or not, we walked in pairs to the rear entrance of the

171

Infirmary. Hilary and Mike led the way, and Theo and I followed behind Jenn and Katie. Huddled together inside of the pauper's room on the first floor, we made a plan.

"I think I have a surprise for you, Rick." Mike said with a pleasant look.

"Really? Did you?" Hilary ginned, giving Mike a big hug, and then looking over to me. "That is... if you want."

"What? What is it?" I asked curiously.

"Follow me." He said smiling, and turning on his flashlight, spun on his heel and headed out of the room and down the hallway.

"Where are we headed?" I asked another question, wondering if I would get a response.

"The collapsed area." Mike said over his shoulder.

I could hear gasps, murmurs and whispers from in front of and behind me. My head spun remembering the terrifying moments when my life flashed before my eyes. I wondered what he could have discovered that would be a surprise to me, and what could Hilary have meant by '...if you want.'? I had an expected adrenaline rush when we arrived at the Infirmary, but now my heart was racing excessively. After walking a bit, I could begin to see the rubble, dimly in the distance. I began breathing deeper and more rapidly, unsure if I was ready to face the devastation that I had tried so desperately to escape from on our first visit. What was once a part of the corridor and an outside room, were now a pile of debris... concrete, re-bar, and bricks.

"I hope it's here." Hilary said as she and Mike began to climb through the remains of the collapse.

"If not, I'm gonna kill Tim. He said it would be." He began to search the area with his flashlight. We had all entered the space and I could hear the girls draw a deep breath. My eyes followed the beam of light along with Mike.

"Whoa..." Katie let out.

"No kidding. The pictures don't do it justice." Jenn agreed.

"It's here!" Mike shouted, holding the light steady, pointing it just beyond where the exterior wall once stood. Something large and aluminum-silver caught my eye.

"Give me a hand Rick." He said, walking towards the 'thing'.

This thing, as it turned out was an extension ladder. Being aluminum, it was lightweight, and we had no troubles bringing it inside. I helped Mike to stand it upright and lean it against one of the standing walls.

"How bad do you want to know what's in that drawer?" He asked, shining the light upwards, lighting the chest of drawers that was still upright against the fourth floor wall. Jenn and Katie gazed in disbelief at the fact that it seemed to be hanging almost in mid-air.

"I want to know pretty bad." I smiled, but spending more than two decades in construction, I was very well acquainted with ladders and had my doubts about the feasibility. "Will that ladder reach all the way up there?"

"I think so. It's a thirty-two footer. I guessed it's about thirty foot up, so you won't have a lot of extra ladder." He said confidently, but it was, honestly, not very reassuring.

"Okay then... no time like the present.' I inhaled deeply, trying to overcome my inner fears. "Let's do this."

Theo and Hilary held the lights while Mike and I fumbled awkwardly with the ladder on the uneven piles of debris. Hollow, metallic clattering noise echoed in the cold, empty night as we banged the ladder into place. Mike helped hold the ladder while I began to raise the extension. Again the sounds seemed uncomfortably loud as the rails of the ladder ground against each other and the locks slid into place, rung by rung with a 'scrape- clank'. When I had raised it as far as I could reach,

I began to climb the ladder, pushing against the upper section until it was fully extended. I began to feel off balance, noticing the foot of the ladder was not far enough away from the wall. Quickly, I descended the ladder and planted my feet firmly on the ground.

"We're gonna have to move it back about another four feet or so to get the angle right. Otherwise, it's just going to fall backwards when I get to the top." I explained. Looking down, I noticed there wasn't a good, clear, level spot on the floor to set the feet of the ladder.

"This might take a couple of you to hold this." I said as I lifted the ladder by the lower rungs and drug it backwards to the point where it had the proper angle. There was a fairly flat chunk of concrete that was about a foot and a half above floor level. I sat the bottom rung on it.

"You're kidding right?" Hilary said in disbelief.

"I think he's serious." Theo answered her as I began to step onto the second rung of the teetering ladder.

"Oh god! Somebody grab it!" Jenn yelled out in a panic, as Mike took a firm grip on one side, and Hilary held on to the other as if it were her life that depended on it.

Nearly twenty feet up, I looked down to my friends and said, "Be ready to run if this ladder or the chest of drawers gives way. I don't want any of you hit by anything falling..." I took another step. "...even if it's me."

"Shut up!" Katie was feeling almost dizzy at the thought, while she looked up to where I was.

My hands grasped the top rung of the ladder, which was practically even with the bottom of the chest. All of my training had educated me that I was as high as I could safely go on an extension ladder, but then again, I was balancing the bottom rung on broken bits of concrete, piled on top of each other... so I placed my hands against the sandy remains, where the wall had met the floor, and took another overly cautious step. Now eye level to the handle on the bottom drawer, I slowly reached out and gave it a very gentle tug. It opened slightly, just over an inch, but no farther. My loud exhale was heard by all, and met with replies of 'be careful' and 'easy does it'. Another step and I found myself having to turn my head to the side with my chest against the wall to keep my weight from pulling me off of the ladder backwards.

My fingers were numb from having a white knuckle grip on the freezing metal ladder, but I found myself sweating, and my face feeling flush as I reached over to slide my fingers into the narrow opening of the drawer. I knew the odds were slim, but I nervously awaited a spider or worse a mouse or rat to climb up my hand or even bite me. I steadied my nerves as best as I could, knowing if I was caught off guard I might jump ever so slightly, which would end badly...very badly. The sweat beaded on my brow and upper lip, and chilled me to a shiver when a slight breeze came in through the ripped open exterior of the building. The ladder wiggled the slightest amount and I could hear the groans of my friends below. I said a silent prayer in my head and recollected my composure.

I wedged my fingers between the drawer and the frame of the chest and pried so hard that even the muscles of my face tensed. It was no use.

"It's not going to budge." My voice filled the empty space.

"Maybe something inside is blocking it." Katie's brilliance flowed without a thought. Her little man was now pretty mobile and found mischief where he could "It happens all the time when my little man puts a toy or a book in an open drawer."

My hand slid from its position and I turned it the opposite direction, palm facing the drawer above. Curling my fingers around the brace, I slid my hand from the nearest point towards the farthest.

"Katie..." I called down as my hand stopped abruptly against a rigid object. "...you're a genius. I feel something." That 'something' was wedged upright against the brace, in between some materials, clothes, bed sheets, or something like that. Without seeing them, all I could tell was that they were sturdy cotton. I contorted my hand and fingers in an unnatural and uncomfortable way, trying to dislodge the object. The more I strained, the tighter it seemed to be jammed, until I felt it give, just a tiny bit, but that was enough to give me hope. Feverishly, my fingers began to flail around inside the drawer, thumping and catching the object.

The object finally moved, fell, and the pressure against my hand was relieved. Almost frantically, I began to pull the pieces of cloth from the drawer, bungling through them one-handedly, tossing them to the ground one at a time. There was nothing notable about the clothing that I pulled from the drawer, but when I had emptied them all from the drawer, I felt around to be sure nothing was left in the drawer. Slipping my fingers under the object and clenching it between them and my thumb I withdrew a tied, leather satchel, no larger than eight inches by twelve inches. I tucked it into the waistline of my pants and began my descent. With each step downward, my body began to tremble more and more uncontrollably. By the time I reached the lower rungs, the entire ladder had begun to shake. My knees had gone weak and I stumbled off of the ladder, and had to catch myself from falling. I quickly found a spot in the rubble to sit.

"Did it." I spat out amidst my heavy breathing.

"I hope it was worth it." Jenn joked, in relief.

"I hope so too..." Mike added. "...because we bent the bottom rung of Tim's ladder."

"If we get out of here in one piece, I don't care what's in this bag, I'll buy Tim a new one." I was beginning to return to feeling as normal as could be expected.

"So, what is it?" Hilary's excitement was evident.

"As badly as I want to know, I'm totally afraid I might be really disappointed, so if we can wait a little while, I'd appreciate it... you know... let me relish in this as a victory because, well, because it might not be one." Even though I didn't mean to dull the high we were on, it was a sobering moment for everyone.

Mike and Hilary managed to lower the ladder and stash it back outside where Tim had left it for us to find. We quietly found our way back to the paupers' room where we had begun the night's adventure.

Jenn opened her bag and retrieved two smudging sticks made of white sage and sweet-grass. She handed one to Hilary and one to Katie. Pulling out a box of wooden matches, she struck one, cupped her hand and lit Hilary's sage stick. It took nearly half a dozen matches to get both sticks smoldering well. Jenn placed the matches back in her bag and withdrew two large owl feathers, handing one to Hilary and Katie, who used them to fan the glowing end of the sage to waft the gray smoke. In turn, we each washed our hands in the smoke, then took the smoke in our hands to wash over our eyes, faces, heads, and hearts. When we had all finished the ritual, Theo opened the small shoulder bag he was carrying and passed long white tapered candles with foil holders to me, Jenn, and Mike. He also drew out a large abalone shell and filled it with cedar and lavender. He nodded to Jenn as he pulled out his own feather from a zippered side pocket on his bag. Without exchanging a single word, Jenn grabbed her matches again, and lit Theo's herbs until they too began to billow fragrant smoke into the air. She then lit our candles and placed the box of matches back in her bag, zipping it closed.

"Whoa..." I mumbled, noticing the haze of burning herbs that filled the room with an eerie fog.

"We need to all continually pray, or at the very least think positive thoughts, while we walk room to room, letting the smoke and candlelight into every corner, opening every door, any drawer...everywhere. I always pray out loud, but just do whatever you are comfortable with, as long as it is positive..." Theo gave clear instructions.

"What about helping them move on?" Katie asked.

"We can work on that while we clear the negative energies. In each room we need to guide the souls to the point of light, the place where they feel warmth, love and acceptance." Theo answered.

"And we should also try to let them know they have the power to move on, that they are only trapped by their own fears. Let them know they hold the power to find the happiness and peace they deserve." I added, and Theo nodded in agreement. Jenn, Mike and I went around the room, in a clockwise movement, holding up the candles. We were closely followed by Theo, Hilary and Katie who wafted their smudging smoke throughout the space. Room by room, corridor by corridor, the spaces were cleared of negativity. Theo and Jenn prayed out loud, but in a low tone which began to sound like a ritual chant. Hilary, Katie, Mike and I spoke word of freedom in every individual area, encouraging any spirits to find their peace and move on to where they belonged.

It had been an uneventful evening so far, and soon we had moved from the first to the second floor. Though we had wanted to take a break to thaw out by the time we had finished the second floor, we knew we had to keep going to keep the ceremonious ritual unbroken. The six of us managed to keep a slow pace, making sure not to rush through any room and possibly leave any space untouched by light and smoke, and we entered each stairwell as we came to it in order, cleansing the space up to the next floor and then returning to the current one before moving on. The murmurs of prayers among chattering teeth and the tapping of our footsteps were the only sounds we had heard, and ours were the only shadows seen, even as we finished spiraling through the third floor. The sound of twelve shoes on the final stairwell leading up to the fourth floor seemed to echo louder than any sound we had made all night. Reaching the top of the stairs, the steady concentration of the team was broken by Mike.

"My candle is about to go out. It's almost gone." He noted, drawing everyone's attention.

"Mine too." I said realizing all three candles were nearly spent, drowning in their own wax.

"Shit!" Mike said as the flame dwindled and died.

photo by Hilary Lee

photo by Hilary Lee

EXCITING RUNAWAY.

Serious Mishap to Medical Students Who Were After Material for Dissecting Purposes.

Mr. Brandy Horton, of Seering Medical College, Columbus, came over here, Saturday, with a request from the faculty of the institution for the body of Muddie Taylor, the insane pauper, who was killed by jumping from a fourth-story window at the circumstances

Photo by Rick Kueber

CHAPTER 13
FROST & FLAMES

"I only have one more." Jenn informed everyone. "I didn't expect to have this many burning at the same time. It's in my bag, Mike."

He dug through her bag as if he were searching for air to breathe. He pulled the last candle from her bag and turning it on its side, in his hand, placed the wick in the flame of my nearly spent candle. The light it gave off was somehow calming, and Mike gave a sigh of relief. We found ourselves subconsciously rushing and intentionally slowing down moving from room to room with prayers and smudging rituals. Every step grew colder, every room more ominous. We had begun clearing the shorter half of the fourth floor. As we had done on the previous floors, we worked our way from one side of the collapse to the other. It wasn't the smoothest transition, but as we moved from one side of the cave-in to the other, we would break into two teams of three; one team would remain near the devastation, continuing to say prayers and filling the empty chasm with the smoke of the cleansing herbs, while the second would scurry down the stairs across the main corridor on the first floor and then return to the opposite side of the collapse, where we could see the others. Only when the second half of us returned our thoughts and concentration to the helping and healing of the lost souls of the Infirmary, would the other half of our group follow, catching up to us as quickly as they could.

Having just finished one of the rooms, and being over half way through the entire fourth floor, we found ourselves in the corner of the main corridor and the last wing. Collectively, we paused, somewhat frustrated with the complete lack of activity. We weren't sure if our rituals were actually helping free the spirits or if we were being avoided and all of our time and effort was for naught. Before I could speak, Theo stopped his prayer completely, for the first time since he had begun.

"This is Maddie's room." His voice was calm and low as he motioned over his shoulder to the room to his right. His use of the present tense snapped us all back to the reality that even if the night had been inactive, this place was terribly haunted, without a doubt.

"I'm sorry guys..." Hilary began, "I thought it would be crazy active like usual."

"Maybe it's just poor timing." Mike added.

"Time..." I whispered. "Time is just an illusion."

We entered the room filling it with the sweet and pungent aromas of white sage, sweet-grass... cedar and lavender, and only one of the candles, the one Mike had recently lit, was giving off much light, but the light flickered and shimmered in the foul darkness of the room.

"An illusion?" Mike asked. "Is that relevant, or just a metaphor, or what?"

"Relevant." Katie spoke up. "Time is a liar. It makes us promises that it rarely follows through with. It's important that these spirits understand that no matter what they expected of their life, that their

182

afterlife is not meant to be spent in regret."

"To anyone here, who may be listening." Jenn spoke, hoping Maddie and every soul could hear her. "Katie and Rick are right. Time is a lie and a liar. There is only now...this very moment. The past is not time, it's only memories of happiness and regret and the future is only expectations, dreams and fears of what the present could become. Live in the moment, make NOW what you want it to be. You all have the power to make your own peace and happiness."

"Wow..." Mike whispered to Hilary. "I get it... it *is* relevant."

"You must make the choice to not be held back by the negativity that surrounds you." I took my turn. "Right now, in this exact moment, picture your happiness as your reality. Believe in the peace you deserve. No force in existence controls that.... only you do. Seize this moment as your own; let no one and no thing take this from you. Find the peace that brings you warmth and light, and follow that light to your eternal peace." While we spoke on time, Theo had softly begun to chant his prayers, like subtle background music that brought us all comfort... momentarily.

A strong wind blew in from the corridor, cold and cruel, and despite our best efforts, the flames were stolen from us. In a panic, we scrambled to find the matches and relight them, but the one Mike held was the only one that would light: the others had fulfilled their purpose and their wicks and wax were used up. Theo's prayers grew louder, and we all joined in silently or out loud, as we saw fit. As the room grew colder our prayers and intentions became more intense, and the more intense they became, the colder the room became. Mike fought the ever present wind, and lost. The last flame went out and as if it held some magical power of goodness that had been vanquished, the room fell silent.

"Not good." The chill could be heard in Hilary's quivering voice.

"Do you see that?" Jenn whispered loudly. "I see shadows moving."

"Yes." The reply was hissed, yet came from no one in our group.

183

"Quick!" I called out. "Get in a circle."

Like metal shavings to a magnet, we were all pulled to the center of Maddie's room. Our backs were to each other and our shoulders touched. Harrowing, bleak, shadowy coldness grew around us, contrasting the blacks and grays of the once empty room. The beings seemed to be very aware of our presence and we began to explain, once again, about time, peace, crossing over, and all that we knew to say. As we spoke, a rumbling noise increased within the space. The fear of another collapse broke my concentration, and seemingly everyone's. Across the room, in the corner nearest the remains of the bed, a shadow grew, larger and more oppressive than all of the others combined. It seemed to be watching over them, casting its fear onto them. With every moment that passed, the temperature dropped. We shook from the frigid air, and I began to visibly see frost growing on the windows, the floor, and even on my jeans and jacket. We were freezing, bordering on hypothermia, when our fear had reached its pinnacle. One shadow from among the countless souls that surrounded us came forward. It became less transparent than the rest and reached its frail arms out to Hilary.

"Maddie!" Hilary cried out. "We're here to help you."

The face of the shadow woman became more defined, more physically solid. Her eyes were hollow black and her dark, blue-gray lips were dried and cracked as she stretched her mouth open unnaturally. Though she didn't appear to be speaking, we all heard her eerie voice, rough and squeaking. "Leave now...leave me here."

"But, Maddie..." Hilary pleaded.

"I belong here... I belong to him." Her bony finger pointed to the ebony shadow beast that now filled the corner of the room; its eyes glowing a pale blue.

My stomach knotted, not knowing what to do, and I wrapped my arms around my waist. "The leather satchel!" I thought out loud. I immediately pulled it from its place, and tugged at the leather cords that bound it closed. The decades had taken their toll, dry-rotting them, and they crumbled in my fingers. I tossed back the flap and pulled a few random, crisp papers from inside. Realizing what I was doing, Jennifer dug through her bag and with a click, had turned on her small LED flashlight, pointing it to the open satchel. I sat on the floor and the others joined me, crossing our legs, or kneeling, still facing outwards. I stuck the loose, yellowed papers under my knee, and pulled out a leather bound book. I was consumed with curiosity and sat the satchel down between Katie and I. She searched through the bag and her hand came across a tiny object that had slipped into the corner. Before she had even revealed her discovery, she knew what it was.

"We need Ash." She said aloud, displaying a broken, yet shimmering, silver necklace in the glow of Jenn's light. The LEDs reflected off of the silver entwined moonstone pendant, giving off a faint blue hue. "Ashley Sue Helmach... Please help us!" She screamed out as loudly and clearly as her frozen voice would allow, knowing that the mention of her name often brought her spirit to us (many times unintended).

Without a thought, I opened the book and noticed the first pages had been ripped from it. The pages were filled with hand written words and I began to read it aloud-

(The Borrowed Diary)

May 1893- *First, I must thank Paul Martin Bailey, a young man I shared a few winter months of my life with at the Rochester poor house. We shared many things, including our dreams, our fears and our love. I slipped away, without warning, when the spring thaw came. The pages torn from this diary were his story. Those were left for him. This diary was his too, but now it is mine. I was born Taylor Elizabeth Madison. This is*

185

my story.

My birth was in the springtime of 1863, in the town of Newberry, West Virginia. My childhood was as most. When I was nearly of school age, my parents and the elders of the Church began to frown upon my imaginary friends. For as long as I can recall, I have seen folks of all types and ages, that others did not see. I was told from a young age that they were my imaginary childhood friends. It was on a late summer afternoon when I began a conversation with an actual playmate named Billy Black. I was given looks of bewilderment from the folks around us, asking why I was pretending to talk and play with him. I argued that he was there with us, but his father quickly reprimanded me, certain that young Billy was at Beyer's Pond with his brothers, swimming. I nodded to Mr. Black and slipped around the corner to speak privately to Billy, but he had vanished. Not more than an hour had passed when I heard the news that Billy had been brought back home by his older brothers, having drown in the pond that morning.

I was soon shunned by the townsfolk as being queer, a witch, and even of consorting with the Devil himself. My family could not take the ridicule, and we left home in the middle of the night, bound for a more pleasant future. Our wagon was loaded with each thing we had been able to pack, and within three short days, were in a small town well into West Virginia, called Summersville. The name sounded welcoming, and there we made our home for the next several years.

I had learned my lesson. No longer would I speak of those that others could not see, though at times, I could not be sure which were everyday folks and which were the unseen. Though I attended a local church and school, I became withdrawn.

At ten years of age, I made one of the only true friends of my life. She was sweet, kind, and like myself, she had a gift that most did not understand. When I needed a friend the most, she came to me and gave me one of the few gifts I had ever received. When the town began to murmur of my oddities, I pointed the finger to another, for fear of my family losing its home, once again. At eleven, my indications had caused her life to be taken, and I shall never forgive myself for my selfishness. Much to my chagrin, the accusing whispers in hushed tones grew ever louder. I would not put my family through these trials again, and so I left without fare-wells.

As I passed the edges of Summersville, I paid a brief visit to the place where the life of my only true friend was taken. I peered through the smoky window, and saw her dead soul and fiery stare. I ran, as swift and as far as my body would carry, before I collapsed. She knew my secret, and I knew her's, and for this reason, I knew without knowing, that she was in pursuit and would have her revenge, which I feared beyond all reasoning. Always aware, always afraid, seldom sleeping, I moved from village to town, and took refuge when and where I could for as long as I was welcome, for as long as my fear of her retribution would allow.

When I awoke, shortly after running away from my home, I found myself in a peculiar place. I was very ill and nearly starving when I was nursed by a poor, yet kindly elder woman. Seeing my name stitched into the neckline of my dress, last name first, she spoke to me as 'Ms. Madison Taylor' which confounded me at first. I chose to not correct her, and begin a new life. Though I was many miles from home, the missing girl of Summersville was never spoken of, and I wondered if I was thought of as lost, a runaway, or if my parents chose to abandon me without searching. This was not the first time I felt lost and unwanted, but it may have been the most difficult, which I have never overcome.

Several years and countless resting places had passed me by. It was in my fifteenth year that I met and fell deeply in love with a boy of nineteen named Paul Martin Bailey. His family was well to do, and owned the Rochester Poor House. They had taken me in during the harsh fall of 1878 and I remained at the poor house until the spring thaw, when I began to notice the changing of my body. I was with child, and I could not bear to think of how poorly this would reflect on my dearest Paul, should his family learn the truth. I left without word and did not get far when I was taken in by a wealthy land owner as a servant, and it was there, my child was born. A son, whom I named Jacob Paul. When tiny Jacob was nearly three, we set out again. My peculiarity was more forthcoming with the passing of time, and I knew I would soon be sent away.

With the weather warming, we set out to find our way.

*We have spent days foraging for food where we could, and
spent nights in the shelter of the forests or an unattended
barn as we could. Over the next year and a half, our lives were
utter chaos. It is now his fifth winter, and young Jacob is ill
with the fever. We have not eaten in days and have been found
out, and turned out of the barn where we had found warmth,
sleeping amongst the cattle. The farm hand was harsh and
threatening, but pointed us to the Poor House and Infirmary
just three days walk north. My faith is shaken, but I hold a
hope for the future...*

I had only read selections from the many pages of the diary, those
that appeared to have been written in retrospect, in hopes that telling
Maddie's, or Taylor's, story would somehow help. Quite to the contrary,
the situation seemed to be worsening. Looking up from the journal, the
room, my friends, and myself were literally frost covered and our lips
were bluing for the sub-zero temperatures. The shadowy beast darted
from one corner of the room to another, as we watched the cold souls
close in on us, inch by terrifying inch. I had not only put myself, Theo,
Hilary and Mike at risk, but I had endangered the lives of Jenn and Katie
as well. I fought with myself in my head, angry at my poor decisions. My
disappointment in myself grew as did my worry for my friends. Worse
even than that, what of my son, should something happen to me? I
would end up as a regretful soul, like those surrounding us. The chilling
souls were so close, I could have reached out and touched them with my
numb fingertips, but one shadow came forward again.

Maddie had appeared to be nearly a physical being, standing right
in front of me. Her horribly disfigured body, discolored, frozen and
emaciated, was now clearly displayed for all to see. Her blue and
blackened hand reached out to me and a wave of feelings came over me,

189

drowning me in the fears of Maddie's life and the unimaginable pain and degradation of her death and afterlife. Just as I thought she would touch my face, her hand raised and the acrid smell of death stung my nostrils. Another step forward and as her ghastly bare foot passed through my folded leg, and the feeling of a thousand frozen blades pierced my flesh. I tried to scream out, but the pain had taken all of my energy, leaving me paralyzed.

"Uh, guys..." Was all that Theo, who was directly behind me, was able to frozenly stutter.

When I found enough strength, I strained to turn my head, only to see another apparition materializing from the hoard of shadow people that filed the empty spaces of the room. A tall, slender woman with glowing amber eyes stepped forward, her golden hair seemed to flow upward, like the flames of a raging fire. The frost covered floor around her thawed and began to steam under her footsteps. She reached forward towards Theo, stopping just short of where he sat. Unsure of what was happening, we felt we were failing and our circle was broken. We created a gap between Katie and I, and between Theo and Mike, splitting us into two semi-circles of three on each side.

"Ash?" Katie said to herself.

Photo by Rick Kueber

CHAPTER 14
FEAR OF THE UNKNOWN

Though we had no way of knowing the extent of the power of the surrounding shadows, and the beast among them, we were instantly compelled to turn our backs on them to see the two female apparitions approaching each other. Their eyes met, peering into one another's soul. My hands shot over my frozen numb ears as Maddie released a shrill and icy shriek. The specters of frost and flame approached each other, one step at a time, as if they feared the other. Now only a few feet apart, with their right arms outreaching, their ghostly fingertips touched for the first time.

Awe and amazement filled us as we gazed at the two. Glowing auras of orangey fire and misty blue winds swirled about the two, like uncontained neon light filing the room with an otherworldly glow. As

191

they touched, a temporary balance was found, the auras grew blindingly bright and then diminished, as did the two apparitions. My mouth dropped open when the glow dimmed and I no longer saw two tormented souls, but instead I beheld something unexpected, like a vision within a crystal ball... a moment in time, long past... of young Ash, alive and vibrant, touching hands with a young dark haired girl, Maddie. The two young girls giggled, and embraced in a waving field of green, under brilliant blue, cloudless skies. There was a kindness, innocence and selflessness in their childhood memory. Neither judging, neither better than the other, nothing to gain from each other but friendship, and that was how it should be. We watched, spellbound, each of us remembering that one childhood friend we could always confide in and trust, who we eventually lost, for one reason or another... sometimes for no reason at all.

The girls began the clapping game as Theo has seen in his dream visit.

"Two little girls so cute and nice,

Met their deaths in fire and ice.

For a hundred years they played in hell,

With tortured souls, where angels fell.

When the dead girls cried the living came,

To free them from the Frost and Flame."

As the girls sang and clapped, the sky in the childhood scene grew dark, and angry clouds overtook the pleasant sky with thunder and rain. Lightning's condemning finger pointed to Ashley, and in an instant of senseless judgment, singled her out... with a thunderous crack of its gavel, sentenced her to death by fire, and misunderstanding. In that exact point in time, fat and heavy flakes of snow began to fall on little Maddie. Her form aged years in mere seconds, and the soft snow became heavy, sleet filled and relentless, as her movement slowed, her skin paled and icy frost blanketed her exposed flesh.

In the midst of our broken circle of friends, within this bubble of imagery, we saw two entities, two strangers, finding themselves as old friends, and then losing themselves again. Ashley had become an inferno, Maddie a frozen, glacial pillar of a woman, both still reaching out for one another's hand, yet their efforts fell inches short. In a deafening moment of finality, like a sudden explosion, sparks, embers, and frosty shards of ice filled the air, and the room. All went black.

The absence of light was so consuming I felt as if I had gone completely blind. It was absolute darkness; a darkness so intense that it physically hurt trying to strain to see...anything. For a moment, I held my breath, afraid to move, afraid to breathe and break the painful silence that surrounded me. I wondered if I was still in the same room, or had I been taken away, somewhere so deeply alone that it was devoid of light, sound, and even life. Where were my friends? Did they wonder where I had gone, and was there still some incredible phantasm occurring at the Infirmary, only I was no longer a spectator, or participant? A flurry of fears and questions flooded my mind in a matter of seconds, but the thoughts at the forefront of them all were these: Would I see my son again and did he know that he was the most important and miraculous thing in my life?... and then there was Tabitha. I had promised myself that I would bare my soul to her, tell her I had feelings for her, or at the very least begin to take steps in that direction, regardless of the outcome, but I hadn't. Regret was my companion when slowly, I began to see... something. My eyes adjusted to the faint light, and a wave of relief came over me.

"Wow! That was intense!" Theo spoke first, followed by what sounded like a collective exhale.

"Is everyone okay?" I squinted in the dim light that filtered in through the dirty window.

"I think so." Answered Katie.

"I'm good" Jenn said almost simultaneously.

"You alright?" Mike asked Hilary, who whispered 'yeah' in response. "We're alright."

There was a feeling of comfort and serenity in the room that I had not felt in such a long time, probably since before my first visit to the Infirmary, I nearly did not recognize it. I had just witnessed one of the most incredibly vivid paranormal experiences of my life, but I could only imagine what its meaning could have been.

"What the hell just happened?" I had to know if anyone had any explanations.

"I thought maybe Ash was helping Maddie, I mean Taylor, cross over, but I don't know what happened really... it was like all of the sudden every entity in the room vanished and took the light with them." Hilary gave her thoughts.

"Yeah, I thought kinda the same thing." Jenn agreed. "I mean... it does feel a lot..."

"Lighter?" Katie interjected.

"Exactly!" Jenn smiled as she tapped her flashlight, causing it to turn on again.

"So, did it work?" I asked. "Are we finished, or should we relight everything and finish the smudging?"

"We should definitely finish smudging since there are only a few rooms left, but I can't tell if they have all crossed over or not, which is odd to me." Theo seemed confused by it all.

Corridor walls degraded by water stains, peeling paint and graffiti, corners filled with spider webs, discarded bits of trash and crumpled papers, and antiquated rooms scarred by memories of sorrow and despair all seemed unchanged and untouched by our presence and our efforts. The relentless efforts of six like-minded, and goodhearted individuals had unleashed everything in their clearing, cleansing, and blessing arsenal. Before the sun had given birth to a new day, our team had smudged and blessed every inch of the Infirmary we could find and had gathered our belongings together.

Leaving the decaying building, we quietly passed through the rear entrance. Twilight filtered through the misty, winter fog that hung heavy in the air. My five friends and I gathered around Mike and Hilary's truck while the vehicles warmed up. Few words were spoken as we packed our belongings into the trunk of the car, and the back seat of the truck.

"Thanks for coming. I think it really helped." Hilary said, but I could sense the doubt in her words. "Do you want to come back to the house and rest up before you head home?"

"What do you guys wanna do?" I was ready to get on the road and get home, but it was a team decision, like all of our decisions.

"I'd rather just get on the road." Jenn spoke up first. "No offense."

"Me too." Theo agreed.

"You're driving, so it's kinda your call... but I just want to be home."

195

Katie yawned.

Handshakes and hugs ensued, but the emotions were at a low. I watched out the window as the Infirmary diminished and disappeared altogether from my view, but I lacked a sense of accomplishment. It was not unusual, quite the opposite in fact, to leave an investigation, or wrap up our final efforts on a case and feel no sense of closure. It was a feeling of emptiness, a lack of worth, and a reoccurring moment when we all questioned our purpose and our choices to invest so much time and effort for so little in return.

The sun rose higher in the cold sky and it brilliance remained dulled. The mood in the car was somber exhaustion, but no one napped. If I had to guess, I would expect that the thoughts of my team, my friends, were considering the very things I was. Why did we choose to do what we did? I replayed every memory I could recall about the history, the visions, and the investigation in my mind, when it occurred to me: The answer to the question was probably the same for all of us... It was never a choice. Our pursuit of the truth and desire to help everyday people, and souls in despair was not a choice, it was a passion and a calling that we could not ignore.

The entire drive home, my mind wandered while the radio drumbled a constant, low stream of music and commercials in the background. I had pulled my friends into a dreadful nightmare, spending their time and money and leaving them with no satisfaction other than a few memorable encounters with those on the other side of our reality. I couldn't help but wonder... Is this how it ends?

We stopped once for a fast food lunch and another time to fuel up and for a restroom break. Even then, we avoided speaking of the haunting of the Infirmary, if we spoke at all. The trip home from any investigation, whether it was a one hour drive or ten, was almost always quieter than the ride there, but mostly due to exhaustion. Today was different. It felt much different than any confusing or disappointing case we had ever had. The norm for paranormal research was actually disappointment. We rarely left with answers, or closure, or a true sense of finality. At best, we might get a thank you from an individual or family who had been given some peace of mind through our help. Only on two specific incidents did we feel we knew the outcome of our work had been successful for the spirits involved, and even then, there was always a question in the back of our minds, a never ending doubt and second guessing.

We arrived at my home, and said good bye once again. I carried my gear inside, packed it away in the office and began to mindlessly search through the kitchen for something easy to make for dinner. I settled on spaghetti: quick, simple, and easy clean up. The best thing about a spaghetti dinner was that it was one of my son's favorites, and he would soon be home. It was hard for me to fathom, but somehow, I missed him more than usual. Every brush with the other side made me long for more time with him and made every minute and every memory with him even more precious.

My evening with my boy was a wonderful distraction, but the evening flew by. The next two weeks seemed to pass so slowly, proving Einstein's theory of relativity. The day to day chores kept my mind focused on other things besides the Infirmary. My nights, on the other hand, were spent lying awake in bed, wondering if I slept, would I have disturbing dreams and visions, and if I stayed awake, would I be visited by Ashley Sue, or Taylor Madison? Night after night, my thoughts were the same. In those weeks, I did not sleep much, I did not dream at all, and I had no mid-night visitations.

***

It was on a Saturday afternoon, about two weeks after I had returned home, when I made my decision to have a moment of courage. I pulled my phone from my front pocket and searched through my contacts.

"Hey... what's up?" The soft voice on the other end was like honey, sweet and soothing.

"Not much..." I hesitated. "I just hadn't talked to you in a while. How ya been?"

"Not bad, I guess." She said in a melancholy tone. "Just working and avoiding people... you know... just being me."

"Yeah, that sounds about right." I smiled. "Well... I understand if you don't want to, but... um... would you want to go for some coffee sometime? I'd really like to talk to you about something."

"I dunno... sounds serious." She teased.

"No... it's nothing serious, I guess, mostly just going for coffee." I didn't want to say too much in fear of being rejected.

"Sure... when?" Her response wasn't enthusiastic by any stretch of the word, but it did seem positive.

"Awesome." I responded without thinking. "I mean, whenever works for you."

"How about tomorrow morning? 10 or so?" She asked, as if I would ever tell her no.

"That sounds perfect to me." I felt like a teenage nerd who had just scored a date with the head cheerleader, even though this wasn't a date, and we weren't teens. "I'll see you there?"

"Yep." She sounded pleased that we were meeting for coffee, and being perpetually ten minutes late said, "I'll text you in the morning... just in case one of us over sleeps or something."

"Alrighty... I look forward to it." I said, as we ended our conversation and thought to myself... 'What a stupid thing to say! I probably sound like an idiot.' This was my typical inner monologue. I was in near constant doubt of myself. I was a roller coaster of confidence... depending on the situation, I was either overly confident, or had no self-esteem whatsoever.

After receiving a text letting me know to meet at 10:15 am, I gave myself a once over and headed out to the coffee shop. As usual, I arrived about ten minutes early and waited in the parking lot until Tabitha arrived. I watched her sporty little Mitsubishi Eclipse pull in to a parking space near me and stepped out of my car. Walking up to the door together, I was in turmoil over what to say.

"You look very nice." I said the first thing that came to my mind, honest and corny as it may have sounded.

"Thank you." She replied with a smile, looking down at her torn jeans, and wondering if it was an empty compliment.

"Love your hair!" Again, being blunt, yet honest.

"I'm not crazy about the darker purple. It's three different shades, ya know?" She had almost always had some brilliant color in her hair; vibrant reds, pinks, blues, and purples. The purple may have been my favorite.

I held the door for her and walked with her to the counter to order. When we had gone out in the past, I had always tried to pay but Tabitha was a very independent woman, and often paid for her own, or even paid for both of us. This morning she had given me the privilege of buying her coffee and a muffin. We sat across the small table from each other and spoke in fragmented ramblings about nothing in particular, and everything in general.

"So... was there something you wanted to talk to me about?" She bravely asked.

'To be honest, I wanted to tell you that I have the biggest crush on you. You are an amazing woman and I am so happy to have you as my friend. I suppose I wanted to talk to you about how you felt about going out on an actual date... ' This is what I had planned to say: this is what I wanted to say: this is what I didn't say. What I did say was, "Oh, nothing really important. I was just going to ask you about the jewelry you make. I was thinking about having something made for my team using some of the semi-precious stones for healing and protection, or something like that."

"Oh, that's a cool idea." Her smile had a look of relief. "I can show you some of the different stones I have and what they are used for, and we can look at different designs and styles. I think leather cord or hemp would be best. It's a good idea to stay with all natural elements."

She pulled a tablet from her bag and turned it on. She began to surf the internet and show me a multitude of different styles of stones and natural beads. We had a brilliant conversation filled with humor, sarcasm, education and enlightenment. Though nothing was finalized, I had an idea of a necklace or bracelet and what kind of stones would work well together. I had arrived that morning with a purpose and intent, but having Tabitha help make something for my teammates was never part of my plan. The truth was that I had made up the idea on the spot to avoid an uncomfortable situation. I did not want to put our friendship in jeopardy, and decided to simply live with my feelings, knowing that I had a friend that would stand by me through thick and thin.

The time we spent together was energizing and always left me on a high. When we had finished, we walked out to our cars and said good-bye. I wanted to give her a friendly hug, but I could sense the awkwardness and knew it would be best if I didn't invade her personal space. I drove away happy to have been able to see her, saddened that it had already ended, and wondering if I had made the right decision to hide my feelings.

Photo by Rick Kueber

CHAPTER 15
WITHOUT US

The countless, lost souls of the Infirmary kept their distance from the half-dozen living beings that roamed the building. The oppressive darkness, an evil beast of negative energy, had instilled in them a fear of the human visitors. This beast had gathered every spirit to it and kept close watch over them and the six individuals that seemed as one energy, one purpose, glowing with light and positivity. When the circle of friends and light had assembled in Maddie's room, the beast decided it was time to end their need and desire to free its captive souls.

Ashley had waited for the perfect time to present herself. This was that time. She had allowed herself to appear to be physically matured to that of a woman in her twenties. The new soul, alight with a fire that none of the Infirmary specters had experienced before, called out to Maddie from across the room. Maddie was drawn to the contrasting soul and letting her guard down, allowed herself to be seen by the living. She stepped toward the warmth of Ashley and the two drew closer together. With each step, they grew less transparent to the Infirmary visitors. The two souls approached the center of the circle of the living, in the midst of their life force, they met. With hands outstretched, they touched and Maddie immediately knew whom she had met. They digressed to their childhood, more than a century before. In an instant of clarity, all of the confusion, heartbreak and fear that had created the life of madness, the life of Maddie, disappeared. Maddie no longer existed and Taylor Madison had found herself.

The two girls traveled back to the day they met, when Ash had given Taylor her mother's moonstone necklace to help protect her, but she had given her much more than that. She had offered her a nonjudgmental friendship. In moments their history passed before them, reliving every second in a flash of memory: the moment they met, every afternoon they spent together (including a time when a boy was taunting Taylor and with a touch, Ashley had set the boy's school book afire), the last day that Ash had come to school... The two girls shared their memories apart as well.

Ashley looked on as Taylor was reprimanded by her parents for her oddity, claiming to see the dead. It was during their harsh words and abusive actions that she broke down and told them about Ashley's abilities to move things with her mind and to start fires with a touch of her hand. She wanted her parents to understand that just because she was different, she was not evil and that she was not the only person who had unique abilities. She had hoped that her parents would come to understand that her visions did not make her someone to be frightened of. A few days had passed and her parents had seemed more at ease.

Just over two weeks had passed when Taylor's parents had told her to stay home alone while they went away for the day to take care of something important. They returned late that evening soaked by the afternoon storms.

"It is done." Her father said to her while he unbuttoned his damp shirt.

"You must never speak of seeing someone who isn't there." Her mother spoke to her, but would not make eye contact and scurried about gathering dry clothes for her father to put on.

"But mother, I do not know when others do not see or hear those that I do." Taylor debated.

"Then you will never speak again!" Her father spat as he shouted at her in anger.

"But why?" Taylor slumped to the floor, as the tears flowed from her eyes.

"That devil girl... from the Helmach farm..." Her mother spoke softly, brushing Taylor's hair from her face with her fingers.

"Yes... the church has rid the world of that witch child." Her father had lightened his tone slightly. "Her soul is free... a cleansing by fire."

"What have you done?" Taylor cried out. "She was my friend."

"No more." Her mother spoke solemnly. "You must not speak of her again."

"Then I shall never speak again." Taylor said angrily. "That is what would please father."

"Do not speak so disrespectfully." Her father raised his voice again, throwing his rain soaked shirt to the floor and striking Taylor across the cheek with the back of his open hand. Taylor darted into her room and threw herself onto her bed, sobbing uncontrollably. In that moment of despair, she had made a decision that would change her life forever.

One morning, a few days later, Taylor left for the school house but never arrived. She detoured to visit a place she had never been. She followed the roads to the edge of a farm she had seen only in passing. Turning up Helmach Creek Road, her footsteps slowed. She could see the homestead in the distance, but the walk seemed never ending. When she finally arrived at the front step, the smell of dampened and burnt wood filled the air and a feeling of nausea overtook her. Taylor stood on the porch and placing her hands on the white painted sill, peered through the smoke stained front window. She could make out the layout of the front room, the remaining furnishings and the stone fireplace at the far end of the room. A charred hole had been burned completely through the floor and the ceiling was burned and blackened with smoke.

The abandoned room began to fill with smoke. Taylor's eyes widened and she made a hissing noise, sucking the air in through her clenched teeth. Her hands tensed and her fingernails dug into the window sill, as a figure formed in the smoky room.

"Ashley Sue! Is that you?" Taylor called out.

For a brief second, Taylor thought her friend was okay and the story of her being burned as a witch was just that, a story fabricated to stifle her own ability. There was no verbal response to her question, but as the figure drew closer to the window, she could clearly see it was her only friend, Ashley.

"Forgive me Ashley. I told..." Taylor's heart filled with terror as Ashley's eyes began to glow with an orangey fire.

The room behind the little blonde haired girl filled with a massive, black shadow and Taylor knew that her friend was a ghost; her friend was dead. Taylor took a step backwards, her fingernails raking across the sill and falling to her sides. A sudden flash of light filled the room as little Ashley Sue burst into flames with a harrowing scream. Taylor stumbled back and fell from the porch, into a small shrub that grew wildly. Its barren branches tore at her dress, scratching and slicing her tender skin. Scrambling to her feet, she raced away from the house, straight into the woods. Her eyes stole glances over her shoulder as she sprinted through the brush and trees. Taylor's ankle caught a vine and sent her tumbling down a hill and into the icy cold waters of Helmach Creek.

***

The vision of the past faded and the shadowy beast, with a swirling wave of its hand he called every shadow spirit into hiding. Ashley took the opportunity to fool her friends. With an explosive phantasm of light and sound, she and Taylor disappeared into hiding with the other souls. Ashley's living friends would soon understand what she had done and why... when it was their turn to cross over into the light. It may be fifty years or more before that time came, but to Ashley, it was no different than the next day.

The two girls had disappeared into the dark recesses of the Infirmary basement with the lost souls, and infiltrated their company. She had allowed her energy to begin to shift from wholly positive towards the negative end of the spectrum. In this way she appeared to be falling under the influence of the evil entity, which gave it great pleasure. The living had gone and days passed as moments, while Ashley managed to touch every soul trapped in the Infirmary, showing them the slightest light, kindness, and hope. Weeks had slipped by when Ashley found the time to be exactly right to execute her plan.

"Gather round." Ashley called out to the souls of the Infirmary. "Draw close to me, now."

"The time for peace and forgiveness has come." Taylor joined in the plea.

"Family and loved ones await you in the light, and long to bring you home." The tormented and degraded souls began to encircle the two girls, drawn by not only their words but the polar opposites of their twin souls; like the yen and yang, light and dark, the frost and the flame.

The negative energy of the beast became enraged, feeling its century long grip over the lost souls weakening. It stretched upwards to the sky above and with a terrible, rumbling wail, put forth a final effort to bestow its fear into the spirits. Winds grew strong and swirled in a vortex around the old and decrepit building. Clouds gathered, darkening the day and hiding the sun. A cold rain began to fall with its stinging drops pelting the cracked and broken windows and walls of the Infirmary.

"Now." Ashley and Taylor called out together, their hands and faces upturned.

"Look to the heavens with us and focus on the light above. The time is upon you to know your worth, to realize your home is not here, but in a place beyond that can only be described as love." Ashley explained.

One by one the shadow souls turned their spiritual eyes to the sky above and just as Ashley had promised, a brilliant point of white light appeared to them. The light grew brighter, larger, closer, and the earth began to tremble in its presence. In an instant of conclusiveness, Ashley threw her hands down to the floor beneath them and with an ear-shattering 'CRACK' a blinding light engulfed them. The air around the Infirmary grumbled, trailing off into the distance. The light had come and gone in a fraction of a second, and with its departure, the darkness had gone and the spirits were free.

***

It was a glorious awakening as so many souls had crossed together. Friends, family and loved ones, some they had never met in the earthly plane but somehow knew as if they had always been together, greeted them with arms open wide and angelic choruses surrounded them.

Amidst all of the joyous reunions, a little blonde girl and a woman with raven hair strolled together, hand in hand. Through a vale of ethereal mists, they traveled.

"Thank you for your help and forgiveness." Taylor said, her own voice sounded odd, yet heavenly to her.

"There was nothing to forgive." Little Ashley smiled. "Everything that happens, be it good or bad, has a purpose that serves the good of the universe."

"I understand... completely." This was not just a polite gesture. Taylor was beginning to understand everything with an unfathomable lightness of being, an all-encompassing perception.

"It is I who should have apologized to you." Ashley spoke to her old friend. "It was a misunderstanding and my appearance through the window that frightened you into running away and caused the pain during your time on earth."

"Misunderstanding?" As the word left Taylor's lips, she knew. It was not her doing, not her telling, that had caused the witch hunt of Ashley Sue Helmach. The Church of the Chosen had marked her and planned her death as an example of the power of their congregation, and it was the fear and heartbreak of Ashley's own father that allowed the travesty to occur. "Bless you dear friend. I have missed you for far too long."

The two embraced and the illusions of their pasts were erased as if no ill feelings had ever existed. Releasing each other, Taylor noticed a host of others had gathered around them. The girls were first approached by two individuals holding hands, an adult and a child. A heavenly light shone from behind them and radiant beams surrounded their silhouettes. Taylor rushed to meet them, instantly knowing it was her beloved Paul Martin Bailey and her child, little Jacob Madison. In the second they embraced, they were a family and Taylor realized that even though she had vanished from Paul's life, and her son had left her at far too young an age, the illusion of their broken family was the most painful deception of their lives. Whether they knew it through these difficult times or not, they were always family. More individuals came forth, Paul's parents accepted her as their own and Taylor's parents welcomed her home. Countless others greeted her in turn, the kindly old woman who nursed her back to health when she had first run away, the man who found her lying in the roadway, and so many friends and caretakers she had met in her travels. Her spirit overflowed with joy at the copious amount of friends she had made, and never realized. Her whole life she felt that Ashley was her only friend, but truly, nearly every person she met cared about her in one way or another and had compassion. It was all quite clear to her now, and as Ashley's parents and the Bettiger family joined them, a seemingly endless celebration began. When a great deal of time had passed, Ashley's mother took Taylor by the hand.

"That is a beautiful pendant you wear." She smiled.

"This..." Taylor reached up, finding the moonstone pendant hanging on a thin silver chain around her neck. "But this was yours and how did..."

"Because it was a gift that meant so much to you... and here, your gifts will always return to you." She explained as she retrieved the exact necklace from her neck. The families joined together, and Paul and Jacob took Taylor's hands and together they strolled into their peaceful eternity.

CHAPTER 16
A CLEANSING BY FIRE

On a stormy afternoon, a few weeks after returning home, the team had met for coffee and to discuss our futures. It seemed that our lives were headed in separate directions. The investigations and experiences we had been through had changed us. The scars of our encounters had left us unable to return to the people we had once been, but the truth was that we all had been left with an empty feeling inside and desired nothing more than to be the people we used to know. It was a sad meeting, and though no one really said 'I'm leaving the team' we could feel the detachment in our hearts. Our conversations were a bit heavy and lacking. Just when I thought I could not take the oppressive sadness that engulfed us, my phone rang.

"Hey Hilary. What's up?" I wondered if her haunting nightmares had returned.

"Hey..." I could hear a deep sorrow in her voice. "You aren't going to believe this."

"What? Is everything okay?" I turned the speaker phone on and laid my phone on the table between us. "I'm with the team and you're on speaker." I informed her.

"Hell no, everything is not okay. It's storming like hell here right now." She was distressed, but I could tell it was more than just a bad storm that had her upset.

"It's storming here too." Jenn chimed in.

"Are you okay? Is there a tornado warning or anything?" Katie asked.

"Hey girls..." Hilary acknowledged them. "No, it's not that... It's the Infirmary. Pull up our Facebook page and you'll see."

I looked back and forth at my team for help. I could only imagine what could be going on. There had been rumors of it being sold and even worse, being condemned.

"Hang on..." Theo pulled out his oversized phone and opened up the app. "Okay... here's the page... um... what am I looking... Holy... is this for real?" we all looked over to see the concrete, stone and brick structure billowing flames through the rooftop and from every window.

"I'm afraid so." Hilary's voice quivered and I could sense that she had been crying. "They are claiming it was a massive lightning strike that started the fire, but it doesn't make any sense. It's been raining almost every day since you left and there isn't that much that would really burn, ya know?"

"Do you think the spirits of the Infirmary are still there Theo?" I asked.

"It's all clouded to me. I don't feel like they are there anymore, but it doesn't feel definite." He answered, and I could tell the confusion of it added to his desire to distance himself from the team, at

212

least for a while.

"Do you all think you could come back up and do a blessing on the whole property?" Hilary asked.

"One more for old time's sake?" I asked my friends, and all agreed to try to make it happen.

"Good... because I found something that you might want to know." Hilary began. "I know where Taylor's son is buried..."

"I think I might know where the boy was buried too... maybe." I added, thinking back to the dream my team and I had shared.

We chatted a bit longer but soon we found that we all had to go for one reason or another. My friends and I remained in touch over the next month as we tried to decide on a date to revisit the Infirmary. We were deep into Spring when the day of our return arrived. My friends had arrived late on Friday night and I asked Theo if I could put a few things in the trunk of his car; he quickly agreed and popped the trunk open. I opened the trunk of my car and transferred a few items quickly. Jenn joined me and placed a large bag into the trunk also. We had stayed up talking until the early morning hours. At just after 2 am we loaded into Theo's car and began the long journey back to the Infirmary. A few rest stops, one stop for fuel and nearly seven hours later we found ourselves crossing the Mad River in the early morning hours.

"Look!" Katie shouted, pointing out the passenger side window.

"How cool is that?" Jenn said, slumping over awkwardly to look out of Katie's window.

"The eagle has a friend. Do you see it?" Theo noticed.

I looked out of my window and saw the bald eagle perched high in the top of a long dead tree, and only one branch over was a huge white owl. "This has to be a good omen, right?"

"It definitely is." Theo agreed as we left the bridge, the owl

213

and eagle, and the Mad River behind us.

It had been far too long since I had seen this many smiles at once and our morale had felt this positive. We stopped in Bangs at a small diner for a bite of breakfast, where we met up with Hilary. After filling our bellies and paying the tab, we caravanned over to the Infirmary. This visit felt cheerier than any in the past, until we were within sight of the hollowed remains of a once grand landmark. We parked at the farthest corner of the lot and congregated around the trunk of Theo's Subaru. Opening the trunk lid, Theo extracted a large cardboard box and a backpack.

"Whatcha got there?" Hilary asked inquisitively.

"This..." Theo tapped the side of the box with his foot. "... is about three gallons of holy water."

"And that..." Jenn held up the pack Theo had handed her. "... is every herb in the continental U.S., more or less."

"Really?" I asked with smirk.

"Okay... well it's everything we could get our hands on, and more than I've ever seen in any one place." Jenn confessed.

"Where do we begin?" Katie asked.

"I have an idea." I said hesitantly to the group.

"Let's hear it." Hilary coaxed the idea out of me.

"Well, what if we start in the middle of the ruins and spiral outward to the outer edges of the property." I made a spiraling motion with my finger pointed downward.

"That..." Theo paused with a smile. "...is a brilliant plan. Can everyone put a couple of these bottles in their pockets, or carry them?"

Theo opened the flaps on the cardboard box, revealing a dozen twenty ounce bottles filled with blessed holy water and began passing them out. I fit one bottle into each of my jacket pockets, as did the rest of my friends. Hilary opened her shoulder bag and placed the two remaining bottles inside. When we had the holy water distributed and pocketed, Jenn dropped the backpack from her shoulder and unzipped it.

"Check these out." She pulled out a foot long handmade smudge stick. "I made ten of these, so if everyone could take two we can carry them all with us. I'd like to keep two or three of these going all the time."

"I think that's a good idea." Theo began. "I would like to carry one and a bottle of holy water. Everyone else should take one or the other... two of you using smudging sticks... um, Katie and Hilary... and two more using holy water."

He didn't have to call us out by name. Jenn and I knew he was speaking to us. He demonstrated how to flip back the top of the holy water bottles and with a twist tear them off, leaving the rest of the lid with three small holes like a salt shaker. By shaking it back and forth just right, the water would spritz forward perfectly. We walked up to the Infirmary with purpose and confidence. The structure was recognizable in that the exterior walls still stood, other than that, it seemed alien to us. In the mid-morning light of day the once incredibly majestic building was now a mere skeleton of its former glory days. Blackened and charred bricks plumed out and above the now empty windowpanes and doorways. The roof was completely non-existent as was the entire interior of the building. The fire was so intense that even the ornate metal stairs had folded in on themselves and collapsed like a stick of taffy in the summer heat.

It proved to be treacherous as we waded through invisible rubble, buried beneath nearly a foot of ash and cinders, but once inside we set a match to the three gigantic smudge sticks until they smoldered and poured their pungent smoke into the air. As we spun our way through the building, spraying holy water into the hazy spaces around us, we prayed and asked for the building, and the property that surrounded it, to forget the sorrows of its past and for it to be cleansed of all pain and to release all negative energy that remained. Our noses and lungs were filled with the herbal smoke, and our skin and clothes smelled of white sage when we had finished with the interior and began circling the exterior. It was still a bit cool, but Theo had removed his shoes and socks when we were far enough away from the dangers of the Infirmary. He felt a connection with the earth, walking barefoot in the grass and dirt.

The sky above us was a glorious blue and the world was greening around the monotone devastation that was the Infirmary. The further we spiraled out, distancing ourselves from the smell of wet ashes, the lighter and more uplifted we felt. When we had finished with cleansing and blessing the main property, we found ourselves in the far corner of the parking area.

"One more place..." Hilary pointed away from the Infirmary, across the small road from where we stood.

"There?" Katie asked, looking at a small grassy area, surrounded by a black wrought iron fence, no more than a quarter of an acre.

"Yes... that is one of the cemeteries and the only part of this place that is separated from the main property." Hilary pointed out. "The first graves were marked by small metal plaques, but as the funds dwindled, they stopped using markers, and it was rumored that they even stopped using coffins. I think that is where the boy Jacob is buried, according to the time frame of Maddie's diary, but I can't be sure where it is."

"I think I know..." I said meekly. "Though I can't be certain either." My teammates knew exactly what I was referring to.

With the last of our smudge sticks, now mere nubs, but still burning, and the last two bottles of holy water in hand, we crossed the road and entered the wrought iron gate. Without the aid of the snow, the graves were less obvious, but the dips in the earth gave away their locations. Without a word our group walked directly to the center and worked our way outwards until our final lap around the unmarked graveyard, along the edge of the iron fence and along the edge of a wooded area, brought us to a place from our dreams.

"This is it... this is the place." I mumbled.

"Huh?" Jenn could not make out my low ramblings.

"In my dreams... I stood there..." I pointed to the specific spots from my dream. "...and Ashley was here, holding a young boy's hand. I think this might be where Jacob... is."

"That's right." Katie said, and Theo and Jenn nodded in agreement.

Theo handed his smudge stick to Katie and reached into his inner coat pocket and withdrew two small pouches. With the four of us surrounding the shallow divot that scarred the earth and marked the burial site, one to the north, south, east and west, Theo knelt in the center, beginning to pray.

"I am the East, the sunrise and element of Air." Jenn said unprovoked wafting the smoke from the smudge stick.

"I am the South, the mid-day sun, and the element of Fire." I followed suit, and lit a white candle, holding it out to the center of Jacob's grave.

"I am the West, the setting sun, and the element of Water." Though completely unrehearsed, Hilary did not miss a beat, as she doused the grave in front of her with copious amounts of holy water.

"I am the North, the moon and stars, and the element of Earth." Katie knelt down at the head of the grave and dug her fingers into the grass and loose soil beneath, over turning it with ease.

"I am the center of all things, the eternal force of life and love, I am the fifth element of Spirit." Theo reached into the bags and with sea salt in one hand and crumbles of fresh lavender in the other, he sprinkled them all about.

Just as he did this, a warm breeze swirled around us, and the surprising scent of lavender filled ocean air surrounded us. Our spirits felt lighter than they had since before we learned of the mysterious hauntings of the Infirmary. There was still a lack of closure and an unsettling feeling of separation in the pit of my stomach. As true as that statement was, I believed that our work was finished... successful or not, we had done everything in our power to confront the negative entity and offer our help. My team did our best to show the lost souls how to cross the bridge of light from our world of pain and regret to the after-world of peace and understanding. Theo may have had a clearer understanding than the rest of us, but even for him, there were times like this when we stood on the wrong side of the bridge to know if our efforts were a success or in absolute vain. Though the wind had become stronger as it encompassed us, the candle and the smudge stick remained lit the entire time until, feeling we were finished, we stood up to walk away.

"I have one more thing that I would like to do." I was reluctant to tell anyone prior, for fear that it would cause too many other ideas and lead to indecision. "I don't think this will help anything, but I don't know what else to do. Hilary, can we get any water around here? Like a few gallons?"

"Probably. There is a country club just over the hill. Let me see if I can get some." She said as we walked back to the parking lot.

"I still have a nearly full bottle of holy water." Theo added.

"Perfect... I could use both." I smiled.

Theo popped his trunk open and I grappled a large black trash bag and pulled it out, bear hugging it. It was evident to all that I struggled with the weight of it. I began to walk, bowlegged, back to the cemetery.

"You want some help with that?" Jenn asked after my first few graceless steps.

"I got this, but if somebody could grab those two metal bars, and that grocery bag, I would really appreciate it." I grunted out loudly, in such a strain I was almost unable to look over my shoulder.

Katie grabbed the grocery bag, Jenn snatched up the two black iron bars, and Theo closed the truck. My three puzzled friends quickly caught up to me half way across the road.

"You sure you don't need some help?" Theo asked.

"Can you get the gate?" I knew it would be too difficult for two people to try to carry.

Theo hurried ahead and with a heavy metallic clicking sound, unhooked the latch. He swung the gate open wide just in time for me to awkwardly stumble through it. I plopped the black plastic trash bag onto the ground. I exhaled forcefully, shook my arms feverishly at my sides and then began rubbing my biceps.

"That's about all I can do without a break." I chuckled.

"I offered to help." Theo reiterated.

"I know, but once I had momentum, I didn't want to stop." I appreciated his offer. "You can carry it the rest of the way."

"Where?" All three teammates chimed in together.

"Over by the grave site that we did the blessing on." I clued them in just as Hilary pulled back in to the lot. She jumped from the driver's side of the truck and, dropping the tailgate, pulled out a five gallon bucket. Her bowlegged waddle was even more prominent than mine as she struggled to carry the bucket in front of her with both hands on the bail. Jenn handed Katie the iron bars and rushed out to help Hilary with the bucket. With one of them on either side, Jenn's left hand and Hilary's right hand gripped the bail and carried it with ease the rest of the way to the grave side. Theo squatted down, wrapped his arms around the overstuffed pillow sized black bag and wobbled as he stood up.

"Holy crap." Blurted from his mouth as his face began to redden. His steps were swift and purposeful. Theo reached his goal as quickly as he was able and sat the bag down with a thud.

219

"So, you want to tell us what this is all for?" Katie asked, having joined everyone in the corner of the cemetery where the wooded side met the roadside.

"I just thought it would be a nice gesture to leave a small memorial." I began to explain each step as I performed it. I took the bag from Katie. I drew out a hammer and a small, green hand shovel, like one would use to plant flowers. I began digging a small circular hole about eighteen inches in diameter and six inches deep. I motioned to Jenn, who handed me one of the black iron pieces of re-bar which was shaped like the number "7". I hammered the longer end into the ground at an angle inward. I took the second one from her and drove it into the ground at an opposite angle so that they crossed in an "x" shape underground and the short legs of the re-bar ran nearly parallel to each other, about two inches above the dug-out ground.

"These iron re-bar are going to work as an anchor." I said as I sat the hammer down and drug the heavy bag over next to me. Opening the trash bag, I shimmied it down around the large bag of concrete mix inside.

"Oooohhhhh..." Theo said slowly, understanding the weight of what he had carried.

"Can I ruin that bucket?" I asked Hilary, raising my eyebrows to give a cliché look of innocence.

"I suppose so. We have a bunch more of them at home." She shrugged her shoulders with indifference.

I gathered up several of the empty holy water bottles and filled them from the bucket, making sure Theo's bottle, still filled with holy water, didn't get mixed up with the others. I opened the bag of pebble filled concrete mix and began to pour it little by little into the remaining water in the bucket, mixing it together with the small hand shovel. When most of the mix was in the bucket, the cement became dry and crumbly looking. Looking to Theo, he handed me the bottle of holy water without a word being said. Adding about ¾ of it into the mix, I

220

blended it together until it became soupy. I continued to add more mix, and then more of the regular water until I had a bucket that was half full of concrete with a very acceptable consistency. I poured as much of the mix into the hole as I could.

"Can you hold the bucket like this?" I held the bucket at a downward angle over the hole.

Jenn held the bucket as I had instructed while I scraped the last of the concrete from it. Using the little shovel like a trowel, I smoothed the concrete as best as I could. Reaching back into the bag, I removed the last few items: the borrowed diary in its leather pouch, a spray bottle filled with solution, a small nylon scrub brush and an eight inch by six inch metal plate with large threaded screws in each corner. While I pressed the plaque into place, I admitted my lack of a plan.

"Hil, I thought you might want to donate the diary to the historic society, or public library, or something like that." I offered my idea. "Inside the satchel with the diary is the necklace. I'm not sure what to do with it though."

While I wet the surface of the concrete slightly, I pressed the plaque a bit harder, until it was flush with the surface and patted the entire surface, smoothing it like a 'mud pie'. Katie removed the necklace from the leather satchel.

"I have an idea, if no one is opposed to it..." She said mousily. "What do you think about making it part of your little monument?"

"I think that's a great idea." Hilary was pleased with Katie's suggestion. Theo, Jenn and I agreed.

Katie handed me the necklace. I could see everyone's concern when I took the necklace in my mortar covered hands. I laid it out across the cement, just under the metal plaque, with the pendant in the center. I truly believe everyone gasped when I began to push the silver chain deep into the wet cement. Every four inches, I pushed the chain a couple inches deep. Again I played like the cement was a 'mud pie'. When I was finished, it appeared to be just a mostly flat circle of concrete.

"But... what about the plaque..." Hilary seemed heart broken. "I mean... why go to all that trouble to cover it up?"

"This is why..." I grabbed the spray bottle and soaked the surface, and when it began to dry, I soaked it again. Instructing my friends to slowly pour the water from the bottles over the new memorial. I snatched up the brush and scrubbed the surface gently in a clockwise circular motion. When I finished scrubbing, my friends flooded the surface with the remaining water and revealed an exposed aggregate finish, the moonstone pendant half buried in the concrete, bits of the silver chain here and there, and the metal plaque. It was then that the message that was stamped into it was seen by everyone.

ETERNAL BLESSINGS AND PEACE TO TAYLOR MADISON, JACOB AND ALL OF THE VISITORS OF THE COUNTY INFIRMARY AND POOR HOUSE, PAST AND PRESENT. YOU SHALL NEVER BE LOST OR FORGOTTEN.

We were pleased with our day, and felt our visit had fulfilled a purpose. Our chatter rambled on as we gathered up the bits we had brought with us and wandered slowly back to the parking lot.

"So now what? You guys headed back, or do you wanna grab a bite to eat together first?" Hilary asked with hopes we wouldn't leave so quickly.

"I'm okay with some dinner, so I'll leave it up to you all." I said indecisively. Theo, Katie and Jenn shot glances back and forth and mumbled amongst themselves.

"I think we can make time for dinner before we head home." Theo grinned.

"Anyplace in mind?" Jenn asked, having to avoid gluten.

"Long Branch Pizza, definitely!" Hilary's eyes lit up.

"I don't suppose they have gluten free pizza, or anything?" Jenn asked sheepishly.

"Not that I know of..." Hilary sounded disappointed. "But they have really good chef salads... or we can go someplace else."

"Chef salad sounds perfect." Jenn smiled.

"I can't wait..." I said, nearly drooling.

"Yes! I'm starving!!" Theo may have been small in stature, but he could eat more than anyone I have ever met. Hilary gave Theo the address and we loaded into the car and truck.

As we pulled away from the Infirmary for what would likely be the last time, ever, emotions were mixed. We were happy to be closing the door on another case, even if the ending wasn't exactly what we hoped for, and we were saddened by saying a final farewell to such an amazing place. Theo pulled out onto the road and was entering the Long Branch Pizza address into his GPS while Katie and Jenn yacked away about the experiences we all had and gazed out of the driver's side windows at the remains of the building as we rolled down the road one last time.

I glared out the window to the sky over the cemetery, watching a few clouds gathering. Though I only caught a quick glimpse before the small patch of woods blocked my view, I could have sworn I saw a young boy who stood inside the fence and waved to us. Just as my view was blocked, the old cemetery appeared to be filled of the shadows of people, meandering around, and interacting with each other. I looked to my friends to ask 'Did anyone else see that?" but they were all distracted in their own ways.

"What?" Jenn asked. I must have had an odd look on my face.

"Oh, nothing... I'm just gonna kinda miss that place." I

223

decided it was best to let everyone keep what little feeling of finality they had. I kept an eye out of the back window of the car until the Infirmary was no longer in site.

It was over a half hour drive to Long Branch Pizza, and when we arrived, Hilary was already inside and had pulled two tables together so we could all sit comfortably. We ordered our drinks and mulled over the menu, trying to decide what to have. When the waitress came back with our drinks, we ordered an extra large, Chicago style, supreme pizza and an order of bread sticks with cheese.

"I'll have a large Chef Salad with no croutons, please." Jenn said politely.

"What dressing would you like?" The waitress scratched the orders on her pad.

"Do you have gluten free ranch?" Jenn asked.

"We actually do." The waitress smiled.

"Perfect." Jenn smiled back. "I'll have extra dressing."

"Anything else?" The waitress asked.

"Um, yeah..." Theo grinned. "I'll have a gyro."

"Okay..." She jotted down the last item and tore the ticket off of the pad. "I'll get this order in for you right away." She turned and disappeared.

Our mouths dropped when they brought out the monstrous pizza, and Jenn's salad looked like it should have come with a stack of smaller bowls and a set of tongs. We sipped our drinks, stuffed our faces, and carried on with loud conversations and laughter. Every other person in the place must have been jealous, wishing they were part of this phenomenal group of friends. Theo even admitted the gyro was actually pretty good, which is saying something, as Theo is a connoisseur of gyros and all Greek cuisine. We had spent more time than we intended, but we couldn't drag ourselves away from Hilary or the delicious food. Eventually,

I grabbed up the last slice of pizza with 'oohs' and 'ahhhs' from my friends. We were all stuffed, but I just couldn't resist.

"Oh my gawd... I think I'm gonna explode." I said as I slowly nibbled at the pizza slice.

"If you finish that, even I'll be impressed." Theo teased.

"No way... I'm stuffed and I didn't even finish my salad." Jenn leaned back in her chair and rubbed her belly.

Katie and Hilary watched in disbelief as I took the last few bites. With my mouth still half full of pizza, I displayed my empty hands and spoke, just as the waitress came by.

"It... is... finished."

"Does anyone want dessert? We have some delicious cheesecakes..." She tried to coax us, but we all cried out in unison.
"NO!"

Photo courtesy of Hilary Lee

FROST

&

FLAME

Photos courtesy of Hilary Lee

EPILOGUE

As we left the Long Branch Pizza shop, I had one last request of Hilary. I removed one last bag from Theo's car and handed it to her.

"Can you do me a huge favor?" I asked as politely as I could.

"Sure... what do you need?" She accepted.

"In about two weeks, can you go back to the cemetery and clean up the memorial stone and then mix this up and pour it over the top." I pointed out that inside the bag was a quart of a resinous, self-leveling, clear-coat. "This will protect the memorial from the weather for several years... maybe longer."

"It would be my pleasure." Hilary said with a smile.

We passed out hugs and fought back tears, knowing we may not see each other for a very long time, and we had shared an experience that we would never be able to forget.

***

We talked more on the way home than we had in the past. Perhaps it was because our hearts had been unburdened and we felt we had closed this case, or at least it was closed to us. Though there was plenty of light and pleasant conversation, there was also more than enough time to stare blankly out of the window and just think.

Katie was just as enthused about paranormal research and

investigating as she had ever been, but having a young child had shifted her focus. This was not a problem or a bad thing... this was all part of life, and I applauded her priorities. She has remained with the team and though our cases have become few and far between, she would still assist us and investigate whenever she was able, and that was more than I could ask or hope for. My team had been blessed by Katie's unique outlook and insight.

Decades ago, in another state and metaphorically in another life, Theo had studied theater, dance and other performing arts while in college. He had lost his partner and soulmate just before joining our team, and though I believe we were a comfort and distraction during one of his most difficult times, my team was a transition for him. Theo had recently begun to travel the Midwest and had regularly been a guest at a metaphysical seminar in Chicago and was doing well. Not only had he been spending time doing this, but he had also landed roles in several short and feature length independent films. His life was headed in a very positive direction and we were all more than happy for him. His plans included a future permanent move to Chicago. His presence would be missed at investigations, but we would also miss his unique personality at all of our social meetings too.

Jenn... well, Jenn was Jenn. She was the most faithful person I had ever known and we had stuck together through thick and thin. The team had been through its ups and downs, but she and I were the only real constants; however, Jenn had been planning a move to Texas, where her sister and many of her family lived. This had been something she had talked about for a couple of years, but I couldn't help but wonder if the date was drawing near... I was no psychic, but I could sense a change was coming. Jenn had been with the Team since the beginning, and if I asked her to stay, I truly believe she would.

I would never hold anyone back from their family, their

future or destiny. Each member of EVP Investigations brought some one-of-a-kind element that made us a team that was well respected and at times even envied in our field. Each person had their own quirkiness and individuality, but somehow we managed to come together as one when we were called to help, and for that I was truly proud and grateful.

As the greenery of springtime flew by my window, I felt that this was truly an omen of new beginnings and new directions. I had no idea how many more times we would be together as a team. It was a trip of sobering moments and my mind drifted off to another, one of the few people I felt I could really call my friend.

I hadn't known Tabitha nearly as long, or as well, as I had wanted to. We had shared lots of laughs, but she was a guarded soul and I didn't believe she would ever let me past the protective wall she had built around her. Without choosing to, I had fallen for the intelligent, caring and free spirited person I knew, but the truth was that I didn't really know her. Try as I might, I would never get to know her as well as I hoped. We remained friends, but our visits and meetings over coffee had dwindled. We grew apart and that saddens me terribly. When I think of her, I think of a hundred memories, a thousand laughs and eyes that I had become lost in more often than not... but mostly I think, 'I wish I had known her better'.

A beautiful landmark had been destroyed by a raging fire and the hopes of its restoration had been destroyed along with most of the structure. I closed this case without knowing what had become of the Infirmary souls. We were never able to discover Taylor Madison's final resting place, or offer her blessings and last rites. I wondered if there was some greater purpose for her broken necklace; we had been able to return a similar necklace to a young girl when we buried her remains. I had fooled myself into believing that we would find a way to honor Taylor that would feel as satisfying... something that just felt right... we hadn't.

In life, real stories rarely had happy, fairytale endings, and this was one of those stories... but *my story* had not reached its end.

All Team and Individual Bio Photos by Grace Kirsch

JENNIFER

KIRSCH

Jennifer is a 40 something mom of three and with the recent marriage of her oldest son, is now the proud mother-in-law to one.

Jenn's interest in the paranormal began when she was only a small child. Her grandmother's spirit would visit and comfort Jenn, while her father was away serving in the Vietnam War. Though as a child she didn't recognize it, Jennifer had a strong sensitivity to spirit activity.

Growing up in a Christian household, her interest in the paranormal was squelched as a child, but was rekindled as an adult when she found herself living in a house that had a wide variety of frequent paranormal activity.

While living in an actual haunted house, and EVP Investigations was still in its infancy, she contacted Rick Kueber to come investigate the house and was asked to join the group. Jennifer has been the Team's Lead Investigator ever since. Her interest in the paranormal has spread to her youngest child, who wants to follow in her footsteps.

KATIE

COLLINS

Katie Collins was born and raised locally in southern Indiana. Her interest in the paranormal began around the age of 8, when she had her first personal paranormal experience involving the spirit of her Grandmother. Katie joined the EVP team and quickly grew to be an integral part of the group. Known to be the "McGuyver" of the EVP team, she always has a backup flashlight, batteries or spare roll of duct tape in her equipment case (pink of course).

As a level headed and forward thinking member of EVP, she's always looking for an explanation behind paranormal happenings. Katie has also been known to be quiet at times and is an excellent observer, though she can also cut-up and infuse sarcasm in her rhetoric as well as any team member.

The mother of a young toddler, she has a maternal and sympathetic approach to investigating, and is readily aware when a situation needs to be handled cautiously and sensitively.

Like all of EVP's members, Katie is a great asset to the team on many levels, such as paranormal, social, research, and planning, and she can be individualized by one obvious constant... Katie loves PINK.

THEO
KOSTARIDIS

At 41 years old, and a sixth generation psychic with a long family ancestry of intuitives, Theo was born in Athens, Greece. He moved to the United States at the age of 4 and lived in Florida until after college, when he finally accepted his destiny of intuitive arts, accumulating 20 years of professional experience in psychic readings. In 2001 Theo moved to Evansville, Indiana and now resides in Henderson, KY. He has worked various psychic fairs in numerous states as well as New Age and Spiritual Shops. Over the years, Theo started by honing his natural abilities, and then became very proficient in the use of tarot cards, psychometry, tea leaf and Greek coffee readings, and a variety of other tools. Theo has become the talk of the psychic world in Indiana and hosts seminars and workshops at Barnes & Noble and other locales. Theo has also worked missing persons cases with local police departments with phenomenal results.

Working with Evansville Vanderburgh Paranormal on several investigations as well as hosting seminars with E.V.P. as his invited guest speakers, Theo has become an integral part of the EVP family. Being a Trance Medium*, Theo specializes in communicating with those who have crossed over and channeling messages from your spirit guides and angels.

Terms and Equipment:

EMF: acronym for either electro-magnetic field, or frequency. EMFs are generated by many sources, both natural and man made. The human body emits a natural e.m.f., while a cell phone or microwave oven would emit a man-made e.m.f. EMFs are measured with several different devices, and can have a wide range of strengths and 'speeds'. Much like a sound wave, an electro-magnetic frequency is measured by the strength and frequency of its waves. An e.m.f. detector registering a .5 would represent a wave that occurred .5 times over the set length of time and space, whereas it would take an exponentially stronger e.m.f. to register a 1.5 on the same scale.

Various EMF Detectors/meters used in paranormal investigating:

K-II Meter	MEL-Meter	Cell Sensor

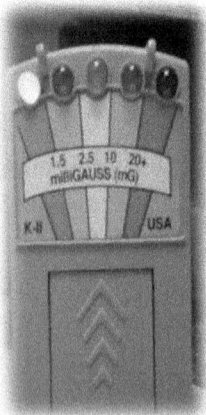  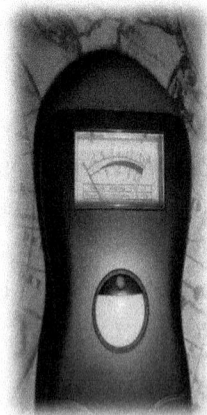

EVP: acronym for 'electronic voice phenomenon'. Many times people experience hearing voices in a haunted location. An 'e.v.p.' is a voice or sound that is not heard by the human ear, but instead It Is plcked up by electronlc means, such as an audio or video recording device.

Often times a paranormal researcher will use a digital recorder to perform an 'EVP Session'. This is a series of standard and site specific questions that will later be reviewed and scrutinized using high tech computer programs to detect any voice phenomenon that may occur randomly, or in response to the questions being asked.

Any type of recording device can be used for these e.v.p. sessions, but a digital recorder records the audio into files that can be easily transferred to a computer for analyzing:

Infra-Red Camera: often called I.R. cameras and 'night-vision', these cameras can film in complete darkness by capturing infra-red light that cannot be seen by the human eye, the video or photos captured by these cameras often has a green cast, or will only be in black and white. While these images are not always the best for capturing shadow phenomenon, they are very helpful due to many investigations being done at night in complete darkness. Many times the un-natural movement of an object has been recorded using this type of camera. A series of infra-red lights can be seen surrounding the camera lens and though they are only seen when looking directly at the camera with the naked eye, the I.R. light allows the images to be recorded into a format that can be seen.

Digital Laser Thermometer: this hand held tool uses a laser beam projected onto any object and reads its surface temperature. It can often be used to detect 'cold spots' and temperature fluctuations which may indicate paranormal activity. It can also be used to find the source of these temperature fluctuations, and at times can prove the opposite: that there is a logical reason behind an apparent cold or hot spot.

Laser Grid : a laser grid is a series of laser beams that can be used to identify distant shadow movement that may not be obvious to the naked eye when lighting is minimal, or non-existent.

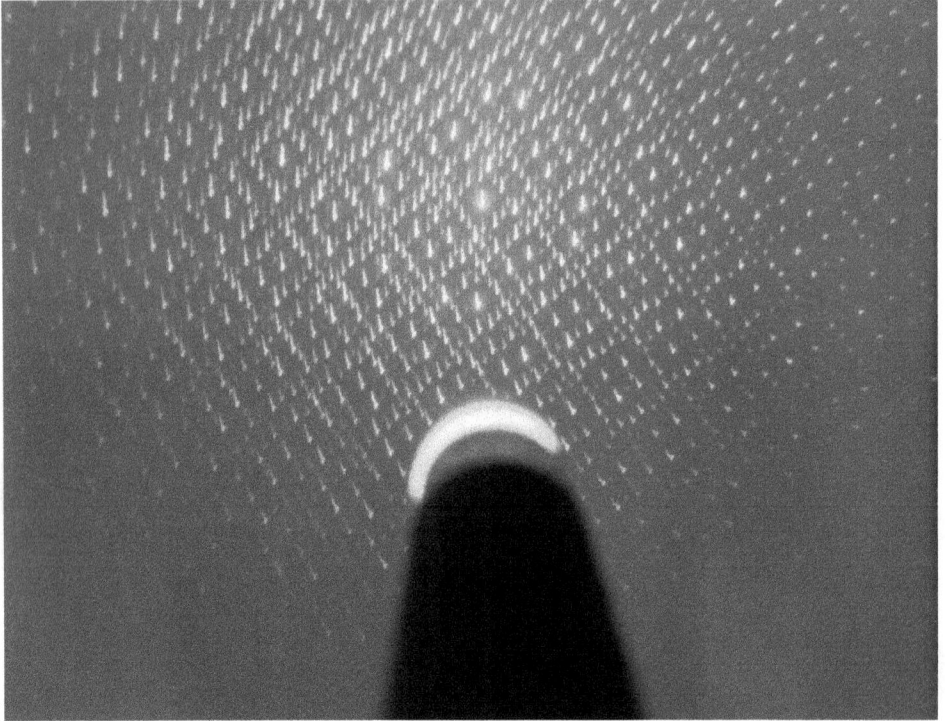

About the Author:

RICK

KUEBER

Rick Kueber was raised Catholic, and has attended many different churches and denominations. He has always had a knack and immense love of science, graduating high school with more than a double major in science. This combination has given him an edge as a paranormal investigator and team leader.

Rick has spent more than two decades in the construction industry working his way from an apprentice, journeyman, foreman, superintendent, and finally, a representative of hundreds of union workers. This leadership ability has been key in every aspect of his life.

Rick has appeared as a guest and speaker at many paranormal events and on numerous radio programs. He has also written smaller published articles.

While he writes about the experiences of his team, Rick says he finds his greatest inspiration and motivation comes from his love and bond with his son Daniel.

FROST & FLAME TRILOGY
By Rick Kueber

What could this team of paranormal
investigators expect to find when their travels
lead them to an abandoned house deep in the
wilds of the Appalachian Mountains? A mere
ghost or haunting would have been a pleasant
experience compared to the horrors that
awaited them, and the truth they would
uncover. Possibly the most puzzling and horrifying aspect of this
investigation was the incredible power and hatred that this entity
possessed, and where this energy came from. The fact that this
menacing fiend had found its way into their lives, and how it had done
so, left these friends and team mates amazed, astounded and terrified.
Based on true events.

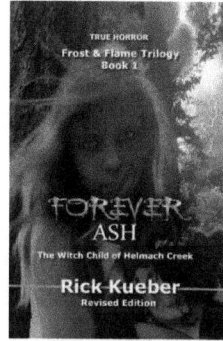

Book 1 Forever Ash: The Witch Child of Helmach Creek

After an enlightening and terrifying adventure hundreds of miles
from their home, the paranormal research team of EVP investigations
was prepared for a simple and peaceful round of investigations to find
more evidence documenting, and proving, life after death. A new
request had brought them to one of the last places they would have
ever expected, a social club. Before the investigation even begins, direful
visitations ensue. A seemingly benign haunting quickly becomes a
curious and frightening mystery that needs to be solved in order to help
the souls trapped in this century old building that once was the home of
the Bettiger family. Ghostly warnings to 'Save the children, before it is
too late' haunt the members of the team, and drive them to a relentless
search for answers, the truth, and to solve the mysterious warning. How
long did they have before it was 'too late', no
one knew, and they had no choice but to try
to find that answer.

Book 2 Shadows of Eternity: The Children of the Owls

Stellium Books

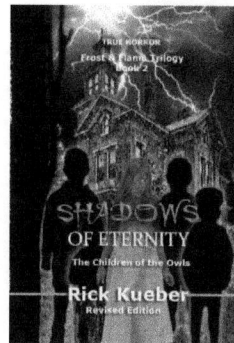

www.ingramcontent.com/pod-product-compliance
Lightning Source LLC
Chambersburg PA
CBHW071417090426
42737CB00011B/1489